SOCIAL SCIENCE LIBRARY   KU-731-261

PCMLP
13642263

ZA
4201
.GoL

THE INTERNET IN THE MIDEAST
AND NORTH AFRICA

Free Expression and Censorship

Human Rights Watch
New York · Washington · London · Brussels

SOCIAL SCIENCE LIBRARY

Copyright © June 1999 by Human Rights Watch
All rights reserved.
Printed in the United States of America

ISBN 1-56432-235-1
Library of Congress Catalog Card Number 99-64033

Addresses for Human Rights Watch
350 Fifth Avenue, 34th Floor, New York, NY 10118-3299
Tel: (212) 290-4700, Fax: (212) 736-1300, E-mail: hrwnyc@hrw.org

1630 Connecticut Avenue N.W. Suite 500, Washington, DC 20009
Tel: (202) 612-4321, Fax: (202) 612-4333, E-mail: hrwdc@hrw.org

33 Islington High Street, N1 9LH London, UK
Tel: (171) 713-1995, Fax: (171) 713-1800, E-mail: hrwatchuk@gn.apc.org

15 Rue Van Campenhout, 1000 Brussels, Belgium
Tel: (2) 723-2009, Fax: (2) 732-0471, E-mail: hrwatcheu@skynet.be

Web Site Address: http://www.hrw.org
Gopher Address://gopher.humanrights.org:5000/11/int/Human Rights Watch
Listserv Address: To subscribe to the list, send an e-mail message to
majordomo@igc.apc.org with "subscribe Human Rights Watch-news" in the body
of the message (leave the subject blank).

HUMAN RIGHTS WATCH

Human Rights Watch conducts regular, systematic investigations of human rights abuses in some seventy countries around the world. Our reputation for timely, reliable disclosures has made us an essential source of information for those concerned with human rights. We address the human rights practices of governments of all political stripes, of all geopolitical alignments, and of all ethnic and religious persuasions. Human Rights Watch defends freedom of thought and expression, due process and equal protection of the law, and a vigorous civil society; we document and denounce murders, disappearances, torture, arbitrary imprisonment, discrimination, and other abuses of internationally recognized human rights. Our goal is to hold governments accountable if they transgress the rights of their people.

Human Rights Watch began in 1978 with the founding of its Europe and Central Asia division (then known as Helsinki Watch). Today, it also includes divisions covering Africa, the Americas, Asia, and the Middle East. In addition, it includes three thematic divisions on arms, children's rights, and women's rights. It maintains offices in New York, Washington, Los Angeles, London, Brussels, Moscow, Dushanbe, Rio de Janeiro, and Hong Kong. Human Rights Watch is an independent, nongovernmental organization, supported by contributions from private individuals and foundations worldwide. It accepts no government funds, directly or indirectly.

The staff includes Kenneth Roth, executive director; Michele Alexander, development director; Reed Brody, advocacy director; Carroll Bogert, communications director; Cynthia Brown, program director; Barbara Guglielmo, finance and administration director; Jeri Laber special advisor; Lotte Leicht, Brussels office director; Patrick Minges, publications director; Susan Osnos, associate director; Jemera Rone, counsel; Wilder Tayler, general counsel; and Joanna Weschler, United Nations representative. Jonathan Fanton is the chair of the board. Robert L. Bernstein is the founding chair.

The regional directors of Human Rights Watch are Peter Takirambudde, Africa; José Miguel Vivanco, Americas; Sidney Jones, Asia; Holly Cartner, Europe and Central Asia; and Hanny Megally, Middle East and North Africa. The thematic division directors are Joost R. Hiltermann, arms; Lois Whitman, children's; and Regan Ralph, women's.

The members of the board of directors are Jonathan Fanton, chair; Lisa Anderson, Robert L. Bernstein, David M. Brown, William Carmichael, Dorothy Cullman, Gina Despres, Irene Diamond, Adrian W. DeWind, Fiona Druckenmiller, Edith Everett, Michael E. Gellert, Vartan Gregorian, Alice H. Henkin, James F. Hoge, Stephen L. Kass, Marina Pinto Kaufman, Bruce Klatsky, Joanne Leedom-Ackerman, Josh Mailman, Yolanda T. Moses, Samuel K. Murumba, Andrew Nathan, Jane Olson, Peter Osnos, Kathleen Peratis, Bruce Rabb, Sigrid Rausing, Orville Schell, Sid Sheinberg, Gary G. Sick, Malcolm Smith, Domna Stanton, and Maya Wiley. Robert L. Bernstein is the founding chair of Human Rights Watch.

Human Rights Watch is dedicated to
protecting the human rights of people around the world.

We stand with victims and activists to prevent
discrimination, to uphold political freedom, to protect people from
inhumane conduct in wartime, and to bring offenders to justice.

We investigate and expose
human rights violations and hold abusers accountable.

We challenge governments and those who hold power to end
abusive practices and respect international human rights law.

We enlist the public and the international
community to support the cause of human rights for all.

ABOUT THIS REPORT

This report was researched and written by Eric Goldstein, deputy director of the Middle East and North Africa division of Human Rights Watch. It was edited by Hanny Megally, executive director of the division, Dinah PoKempner, deputy general counsel of Human Rights Watch, and Michael McClintock, deputy program director. Jagdish Parikh, Human Rights Watch's online research associate, provided helpful comments on the draft. We are also grateful for the generous and expert input of outside readers Grey E. Burkhart and David Banisar, who bear no responsibility for any assertions or errors in the report. Sara Eggerling, Middle East and North Africa division associate, formatted the report.

Human Rights Watch wishes to thank the J.M. Kaplan Fund for making possible the translation of portions of this report into Arabic.

***

Note: This report cites many web pages and web-site addresses (uniform resource locators, or URLs). Since the preparation of the report, some of these may have been modified, relocated, or rendered unavailable.

TABLE OF CONTENTS

I. SUMMARY

The Internet dramatically empowers persons in the exercise of their right to seek, receive, and impart information and ideas regardless of frontiers. Online communication must therefore be fully protected by international guarantees of the right to freedom of expression.

In the Middle East and North Africa, Internet use is growing rapidly after a slow start. Today, all countries except Libya, Iraq, and Syria allow the public to access the Internet through a local service provider. But in a region where nearly all governments abridge the right to freedom of expression in significant ways, many have taken a cautious approach toward a medium that permits persons easily, inexpensively, and rapidly to exchange information in ways that elude state control.

Governments have adopted various means to restrict the flow of information online. Saudi Arabia, Yemen, and the United Arab Emirates impose censorship via proxy servers, devices that are interposed between the end-user and the Internet in order to filter and block specified content. In many countries, including Jordan, taxation and telecommunications policies keep Internet accounts quite costly and thus beyond the means of many—whether or not this is the objective of these policies. Tunisia has enacted the region's most detailed Internet-specific legislation, which is in large part designed to ensure that online speech does not escape the government's tough controls on critical speech in other media. In the majority of countries where Internet-specific laws have not been enacted, legal or de facto constraints on freedom of speech and of the press have a chilling effect on what is expressed online, especially in public forums like open bulletin boards and "chat-rooms" (online discussions where participants communicate in real time).

And in a region where many governments routinely tap the phones of dissidents, Internet users in many countries, including Bahrain and Tunisia, suspect that the right to privacy of correspondence is being violated by government surveillance of e-mail. One Bahraini spent more than a year in jail on suspicion of e-mailing "political" information to dissidents abroad.

Fortunately, some governments in the region have taken a more hands-off attitude toward the Internet—even as they enforce laws that curb other means of expression. This has created paradoxical situations in Egypt and Jordan, where newspapers or articles that the authorities censored became quickly available online without repercussions for those who read, posted, or forwarded them. Algeria, Morocco, and the Palestinian Authority have made little if any effort so far to control online content, allowing Internet users access to a wealth of political and human rights information that the local print and broadcast media cannot publish.

1

This report surveys in a noncomprehensive fashion the Internet policies of governments in the region as they affect the right to freedom of expression. Human Rights Watch identifies policies, laws, and practices that violate or endanger this right. By offering this critique while proposing a set of principles to guide policies and legislation, Human Rights Watch seeks to encourage governments to strengthen protections for freedom of expression at this early stage of the Internet's development.

II. RECOMMENDATIONS

Protecting online freedom of expression requires not only Internet-specific policies that are respectful of rights but also an environment in which free expression more generally is guaranteed. In many countries, online expression is inhibited less by Internet-specific regulations than by pre-existing press codes, defamation laws, and unofficial "red lines."

The right to freedom of expression includes the right to access online communication; the right to seek, receive, and impart information online without arbitrary restrictions; and the right to communicate privately or anonymously online.

To protect and foster these rights, governments should adhere to the following principles in their policies toward the Internet:

(1) Ensure the international right to freedom of expression generally, and ensure that all regulations pertaining to electronic communications comport with that right.

All legislation, policies, and practices, including those that pertain to the Internet, should be consistent with the universally recognized right to free expression. The International Covenant on Civil and Political Rights, which has been ratified by all but five countries in the region, guarantees to every person "freedom to seek, receive and impart information and ideas of all kinds, regardless of frontiers, either orally, in writing or in print, in the form of art, or through any other media of his choice."

Many countries of the region have press laws and penal codes that invite abuse of the right to free expression in various ways. Internet regulations in Tunisia explicitly extend criminal penalties for defamation and false information to online speech; Internet users in Qatar are subjected to a vaguely worded requirement in their service contract that they refrain from "carry[ing] out any activity which is contrary to public order." Jordan and Morocco, meanwhile, have no Internet-specific laws restricting free expression; however, both have laws that curb press freedom, and those laws, such as the ones that prohibit defaming or disparaging the monarchy, narrow the boundaries of what can be expressed online.

(2) Access to the Internet to receive and impart information is integral to the right of free expression.

Governments should take appropriate measures to facilitate affordable access to all without discrimination to online means of communication. For example, Syria, where selected state institutions are connected to the Internet, should move rapidly toward making access available to ordinary citizens.

(3) Censoring mechanisms, if used, should be in the hands of individual users, not governments.

End-users should have the sole responsibility in deciding if and how to filter or block online content for themselves and their non-adult charges. Governments should abolish or avoid regulations that empower official agencies to block online content.

Users, if they wish, can choose from a wide range of free or inexpensive software ("censorware") that filters content accessed from the World Wide Web. They can also purchase modem locks and other devices to prevent unsupervised access by their children.

The governments of Tunisia, Bahrain, Iran, and the United Arab Emirates are among those that block selected web sites dealing with politics or human rights, thus preventing users in their respective countries from accessing them. This form of censorship violates the rights of people to receive and impart information and should be halted immediately.

(4) Common data carriers, such as Internet service providers, generally should not be liable for Internet content.

Laws assigning liability for online content should target the content *originator* (for example, the author) and not the *carrier* or *conduit* (such as the Internet service provider or owner of a computer through which content was transmitted). Laws targeting ISPs impose a heavy and perhaps technically impossible burden on the data carrier, one that is incompatible with protecting the right to freedom of expression online.

Tunisia requires ISPs to designate a director who "assumes responsibility, in accordance with the...press code, for the content of pages and Web pages and sites that the ISP is requested to host on its servers." The decree states that ISPs must allow nothing to "remain" on their servers that harms "public order and good morals." This type of legislation runs counter to the principle of free expression online by imposing a regulatory burden on ISPs that—to the extent that it is even feasible given the nature of data flow online—forces them into the role of censors on behalf of the state.

(5) Strong encryption should be available to individuals.

Individuals should be able to send and receive encoded or encrypted communications. They should not be compelled to obtain authorization to do so; nor should they be compelled to provide in advance to third parties access to encoding "keys" or other mechanisms that would permit the decoding of their communications. Countries that currently bar unauthorized encryption include Israel, Saudi Arabia, and Tunisia.

(6) Government surveillance of electronic communications should not infringe unduly on the right to privacy and other civil rights, and should be subject to the requirements of due process and judicial supervision.

One argument against controls on encryption is that governments retain other effective law enforcement tools, such as surveillance, search, and seizure. However, these should always be used in conformity with international human rights law and the requirements of due process. In particular,

- Investigations or surveillance in public online forums should adhere to international standards protecting the rights to freedom of association and political activity. Such guidelines should be made public.

- Governments should not monitor individual Internet users for civil or criminal investigatory purposes or collect information on the way they use the Internet, except pursuant to a judicial process and judicial oversight that is consistent with internationally recognized principles of privacy.

- Governmental searches or seizure of electronic communications should be conducted pursuant to legally authorized procedures that require there to be sufficient evidence that the user is engaged in illegal activity to justify the search. Any such search should be conducted under judicial supervision.

- Any search should be narrow in its scope and effect.[1]

(7) Individuals should have the right to communicate and receive information anonymously.

Regulations should not unreasonably require identification of persons when they access the Internet or exchange information and opinions online. ISPs should, wherever practicable, preserve the right of users to access the Internet anonymously.

Legislation in Tunisia requires Internet service providers to submit the names of their clients to the government on a monthly basis. Such a disclosure requirement constitutes by its sweeping nature a violation of the right to seek, receive, and impart ideas anonymously.

---

[1] These recommendations are adapted from the Open Internet Policy Principles, which were adopted by a panel of experts in 1997 as a blueprint for policy-makers, <www.soros.org/principles.html> and <www.soros.org/news.html>.

III. LEGAL STANDARDS PERTAINING TO ONLINE FREEDOM OF EXPRESSION

The Internet represents a major development in enabling persons to communicate with others and to obtain information. Some have compared its importance to the invention of the printing press.

In the view of Human Rights Watch, the rights to freedom of expression, information, privacy, and free association under international law apply as much to online communication as to other forms of individual communication. While international treaties and instruments do not address electronic speech specifically, their assertion of the right to "seek, receive and impart information and ideas *through any media and regardless of frontiers*" (emphasis added) is clearly applicable to expression via the Internet.

Article 19 of the Universal Declaration of Human Rights proclaims:

Everyone has the right to freedom of opinion and expression; this right includes freedom to hold opinions without interference and to seek, receive and impart information and ideas through any media and regardless of frontiers.

Article 19 of the International Covenant on Civil and Political Rights (ICCPR) reaffirms that everyone's right to freedom of expression "shall include the freedom to seek, receive and impart information and ideas of all kinds, regardless of frontiers, either orally, in writing or in print, in the form of art, or through any other media of his choice." Article 19 states, furthermore, that restrictions on this right "shall only be such as are provided by law and are necessary: (a) For respect of the rights or reputations of others; (b) For the protection of national security or of public order (*ordre public*), or of public health or morals."[2] The ICCPR has been

---

[2] The Johannesburg Principles on National Security, Freedom of Expression and Access to Information, put forward on October 1, 1995 by a group of experts in international law, national security, and human rights, state that restrictions on freedom of expression should be permitted only when "the government can demonstrate that the restriction is prescribed by law and is necessary in a democratic society to protect a legitimate national security interest" (Principle 1.1, section d). According to the Principles, the burden of demonstrating the validity of the restriction rests with the government. Criticism of the government or its leaders is protected. In addition, a government must demonstrate that "the restriction imposed is the least restrictive means possible for protecting that interest" (Principle 1.3,

ratified by Algeria, Egypt, Iran, Iraq, Israel, Jordan, Lebanon, Kuwait, Libya, Morocco, Syria, Tunisia, and Yemen. It has not been ratified by Bahrain, Oman, Qatar, Saudi Arabia, and the United Arab Emirates.[3]

The Open Internet Policy Principles, declared in March 1997 by a working group of European and North American experts, point out:

> The Internet does not exist in a legal vacuum. For the most part, existing laws can and should regulate conduct on the Internet to the same degree as other forms of conduct. Such laws may differ from country to country, but should conform with the applicable binding human rights obligations contained in the Universal Declaration of Human Rights, the International Covenant on Civil and Political Rights and the European Convention on Human Rights.

Under international law, governments are allowed to restrict the free flow of information to protect certain narrow interests such as national security or public morals. But any prior censorship of material before it is published should be subjected to the strictest level of scrutiny in line with international standards, which normally includes inquiry into the interest sought to be protected, the seriousness of the threat, and whether there are alternate means of protecting that interest that are less restrictive of the right to free expression. Indeed, the American Convention on Human Rights states in Article 13 that the right to freedom of expression "shall not be subject to prior censorship." Filtering or blocking access to Internet material by a government amounts to pre-publication censorship. Virtually all governments in the Middle East that block content on the Internet suppress some material that is unquestionably legal. Moreover, none of the governments in the region make public how censorship is actually practiced and what sites are blocked, insulating their actions from any scrutiny or evaluation under international human rights standards. The decision of what to block, and what technology to use to block it, should be in the hands of end users, rather than governments. A variety of software programs is readily available to users for this purpose.

---

section b). Copies of the Johannesburg Principles are available from Article 19 in London and at <www.osi.hu/colpi/a19>.

[3] For a list of countries that have ratified the ICCPR, see <www.un.org/depts/treaty/>.

The Right to Privacy

The freedom from arbitrary and unlawful interference with one's privacy and correspondence is protected in international law, and applies to electronic communications.[4] A capricious, unjust or disproportionate interference would be "arbitrary," as would one that was for a purpose inimical to the protection of human rights more generally, such as inhibiting peaceful dissent. States may not randomly or freely intercept or monitor e-mail or Internet usage; in the narrow circumstances where surveillance can be justified, it must be subject to limitation and control to avoid infringing these rights. Moreover, the International Covenant on Civil and Political Rights requires states to act positively to protect individuals from such interference with privacy or correspondence on the part of third parties such as non-state actors.[5] Encryption, as a technology that protects communications and correspondence from arbitrary interference, should be lawful and accessible to individual users.

The Right to Communicate Anonymously

Free expression encompasses a right to communicate anonymously. Anonymity in communications is critical to the right to express political beliefs, and to seek and impart information without fear of retribution. Anonymity has served persons who wish to provide anonymous tips to journalists or "blow the whistle" on improprieties in their workplace, authors who wish to write under assumed names, and participants in sensitive discussions, such as an AIDS support group. The role of anonymous speech in fostering freedom of expression was eloquently defended thus:

> Despite readers' curiosity and the public's interest in identifying the creator of a work of art, an author generally is free to decide whether or not to disclose her true identity. The decision in favor of anonymity may

---

[4] The Universal Declaration of Human Rights affirms in Article 12, "No one shall be subjected to arbitrary interference with his privacy, family, home or correspondence." The International Covenant on Civil and Political Rights states in Article 17, "No one shall be subjected to arbitrary or unlawful interference with his privacy, family, home or correspondence..." The language of this provision is broad enough to encompass online communications, including electronic mail and newsgroup postings.

[5] The ICCPR, article 17(2), states, "Everyone has the right to the protection of the law against such interference or attacks." See also Manfred Nowak, *U.N. Covenant on Civil and Political Rights: CCPR Commentary* (Kehl: N.P. Engel, 1993), pp. 289-290.

be motivated by fear of economic or official retaliation, by concern about social ostracism, or merely by a desire to preserve as much of one's privacy as possible. Whatever the motivation may be, at least in the field of literary endeavor, the interest in having anonymous works enter the marketplace of ideas unquestionably outweighs any public interest in requiring disclosure as a condition of entry.[6]

Encryption

Encoding electronic communications ("encryption"[7]) is growing more commonplace, and indeed, is commonly recognized as essential to facilitating the growth of electronic commerce. "Strong" encryption software, that is, coding that is nearly impossible for third parties to decipher, is widely available now to individuals and businesses, where once it was solely used by governments. Encryption protects privacy of communications, but even more importantly, it enables the free expression of ideas and information, particularly where there has been a record of government surveillance and repression. By guaranteeing privacy of communications and authenticating the identity of communicators, encryption also enables free association between individuals in cyberspace, an important extension of a traditional right in the new circumstances of globalization.

While there are legitimate law enforcement concerns that must be taken into account in any national policy on encryption, there is no justification for either banning individual use of encryption or licensing users. Encryption should be viewed as a vehicle of expression like a language; the use of encryption alone should not subject an individual to criminal sanction, any more than should the use of Esperanto or Swahili to communicate.[8] Individuals should not be required to obtain authorization from the authorities in order to send or receive encrypted communications, nor should they be compelled to provide in advance to law enforcement authorities access to key recovery or other mechanisms that would

---

[6] Excerpted from the decision of the U.S. Supreme Court in *MacIntyre v. Ohio Elections Commission*, 514 U.S. 334 (1995).

[7] Encryption involves encoding a text prior to transmission, through the use of mathematical logarithms, so that it can be read only by the sender and the intended recipient, who are in possession of "keys" that decrypt the encoded text and present it in its original form.

[8] Dinah PoKempner, "Briefing Paper: Encryption in the Service of Human Rights," August 1, 1997, <http://www.aaas.org/spp/dspp/cstc/briefing/crypto/dinah.htm>.

permit the decoding of their communications. These are all over-broad policies that penalize law-abiding persons.

Assigning Liability for Online Content

The right to free expression is best served by laws that focus liability for speech on the originator of the offending content, rather than on its conduit. ISPs do not fit neatly into any existing media paradigm and should not be subjected to regulatory structures that may be suitable for other technologies or media, such as a newspaper that can be held liable for articles appearing in its pages. ISPs act most of the time merely as conduits of information (data carriers, akin to telephone companies), offering the technical means for users to receive and disseminate information. In most cases, ISPs have no knowledge of the content of the messages they transmit, or even of the web sites they host—many of which are revised daily by their authors. The situation is arguably different when the offending content is contained in material over which the ISP exercises editorial control, such as a proprietary opinion column; or when the ISP is made aware that offending content has been posted on a web site it hosts and does not remove it.

To hold ISPs presumptively liable for all content they host or carry would pose a regulatory burden on providers that would drastically reduce and slow the flow of information—if the burden could be carried at all. The Global Internet Liberty Campaign (GILC) argues, "No one can monitor the enormous quantity of network traffic, which may consist of hundreds of thousands of e-mails, newsgroup messages, files, and Web pages that pass through in dozens of text and binary formats, some of them readable only by particular proprietary tools." Second, GILC points out, "ISPs cannot provide material in one country while blocking it in another; such a distinction would require an enormous new infrastructure on top of the current network."[9]

---

[9] Global Internet Liberty Campaign, *Regardless of Frontiers: Protecting the Human Rights to Freedom of Expression on the Global Internet* (Washington, DC: Center for Democracy and Technology, September 1998), pp. 30-31. GILC is a coalition of organizations, including Human Rights Watch, that seeks to promote free expression, privacy, and other rights in online communications. *Regardless of Frontiers* is also at <www.gilc.org/speech/report>.

IV. INTRODUCTION

This report surveys the evolving policies of governments in the Middle East and North Africa affecting the right of persons to receive and impart information through the Internet. [10] It aims to reinforce and expand online freedoms not only by identifying violations of free expression rights that have taken place, but also by proposing—at a time when Internet laws and policies are being developed—steps governments should take to protect and enhance the rights of all persons to exchange information and ideas freely through this medium.[11]

In a region where torture is commonplace and free elections the exception, the issue of Internet speech may seem low on the human rights agenda. It may also appear to be an elitist concern in countries where illiteracy is rampant and the cost of a personal computer and perhaps even a telephone is beyond the reach of most households.

But it is arguably in less-developed and in more repressive countries that the Internet can have the greatest impact. Wherever it is accessible, the Internet has provided dramatic new possibilities for people to obtain and exchange information locally and internationally. It has been hailed by many as a force for eroding authoritarian political control and aiding participatory democracy.

As the first truly "mass" medium, one that is inherently open and decentralized, the Internet can enable anyone to receive and to disseminate alternatives to state-controlled information at a low cost. While few individuals and groups have the means to publish books or newspapers, make a film, or air a radio or television program, any person with access to a personal computer and modem can communicate with a huge international audience. A connection to the Internet

---

[10] The Internet is a worldwide network of computer networks that permits any two computers in the system to exchange data via such means as electronic mail ("e-mail"), the World Wide Web, newsgroups (electronic "bulletin boards"), file transfers, and real-time "chat rooms." When used in this fashion, "Internet" is capitalized; "internet" in lower-case refers to a local network of computers that communicate with one another using a common communications protocol.

[11] This report builds on the findings of Human Rights Watch, "Silencing the Net: The Threat to Freedom of Expression On-line," *A Human Rights Watch Report*, vol. 8, no. 2, May 1996; and Human Rights Watch, "Electrifying Speech: New Communications Technologies and Traditional Civil Liberties," *A Human Rights Watch Report*, vol. 4, no. 5, July 1992.

can increase access to information in less-developed countries by putting within easy reach one of the world's great repositories of information, much of it free and continuously updated, and by making that information more easily manageable and transferable.

Such benefits do not depend on a large number of persons having the means to purchase their own equipment and Internet accounts. A government policy of making computers available to the public at libraries, schools or community centers, or the presence of privately run "Internet cafés" or "cybercafés" (shops offering the public fee-for-use Internet access), can help to democratize use of the Internet even in relatively poor countries.

In light of the Internet's vast potential for empowering people to exercise the right to free expression, some have argued that governments have an affirmative obligation to facilitate Internet access for all segments of the population on terms of nondiscrimination. Some have also contended that the Internet can significantly assist governments in enabling citizens to exercise the right, under article 25(a) of the International Covenant on Civil and Political Rights, "to take part in the conduct of public affairs, directly or through freely chosen representatives." The exercise of this right is enhanced by providing citizens access to all draft and effective laws, transcripts of parliamentary debates, and other information relevant to civic affairs. As the Global Internet Liberty Campaign (GILC) notes, "In almost every country in the world, most government information is now created by word processing, meaning that the information is already digitized...[and] can be rapidly and inexpensively put on-line, even using simple Gopher technology."[12]

The Internet's potential contribution to democratic and participatory politics is gaining recognition. In his 1998 report to the U.N. Commission on Human Rights, the Special Rapporteur on the promotion and protection of the right to freedom of opinion and expression outlined the case against government regulation of Internet access and content as follows:

> [T]he new technologies and, in particular, the Internet, are inherently democratic, provide the public and individuals with access to information and sources and enable all to participate actively in the communication process. The Special Rapporteur also believes that action by States to impose excessive regulations on the use of these technologies and, again, particularly the Internet, on the grounds that control, regulation and denial of access are necessary to preserve the moral fabric and cultural identity

---

[12] *Regardless of Frontiers,* pp. 7-8.

of societies is paternalistic. These regulations presume to protect people from themselves and, as such are inherently incompatible with the principles of the worth and dignity of each individual.[13]

Internet connectivity is of special significance to civil society. Computer networks fill a "media gap" between interpersonal communication facilitated by telephone, telegram, and letters, and mass communication facilitated by radio, television, and print media.[14] Computer networks can greatly facilitate small-group participation—within groups, between groups, and between groups and their constituencies—and thus help to strengthen the forces of civil society. Many human rights organizations have embraced the Internet as a means of exchanging information quickly and cheaply.[15] Groups in the Middle East and North Africa have proved no exception to this trend.[16]

In preparing this report, Human Rights Watch sent a uniform letter to the governments of Morocco, Algeria, Tunisia, Libya, Egypt, Israel, the Palestinian Authority, Lebanon, Jordan, Syria, Iraq, Kuwait, the United Arab Emirates, Saudi Arabia, Qatar, Oman, and Yemen. In most instances, the letter was sent to more than one official address, and followed up with phone calls or faxes. The letter contained a series of questions about Internet policies. It is reprinted in Appendix B. Written responses were received from the governments of Jordan, Tunisia, Yemen, and Iraq. The governments of Morocco, Kuwait, Qatar, and the United Arab Emirates furnished limited information about the Internet in their countries. Algeria, Bahrain, Libya, Egypt, Israel, Lebanon, Syria, Saudi Arabia, and Oman

---

[13] United Nations Economic and Social Council, "Report of the Special Rapporteur, Mr. Abid Hussain, submitted pursuant to Commission on Human Rights resolution 1997/26" (New York: United Nations, 1998), E/CN.4/1998/40.

[14] See Andrea Kavanaugh, *The Social Control of Technology in North Africa: Information in the Global Economy* (Westport, Connecticut: Greenwood, 1998), p. 5.

[15] A useful resource is Stephen A. Hansen, *Getting Online for Human Rights: Frequently Asked Questions and Answers about Using the Internet in Human Rights Work* (Washington, D.C.: American Association for the Advancement of Science, 1998). The full text of the printed version can be found at <http://shr.aaas.org/online/cover.htm>.

[16] See Nancy Gallagher, "Middle East and North Africa Human Rights Activism in Cyberspace, *Middle East Studies Association Bulletin*, vol. 31, no. 1, July 1997, <http://w3fp.arizona.edu/mesassoc/Bulletin/gallegh.htm>.

provided no answer whatsoever; the Palestinian Authority acknowledged receipt of Human Rights Watch's letter but did not respond to its content.   The official responses to the Human Rights Watch letter have been excerpted below in the Country Profiles section and reprinted in Appendix C.

The Country Profiles section of this report describes government policies affecting online freedom of expression in eight countries. As the first study of this subject by Human Rights Watch's Middle East and North Africa division, this report is by no means a comprehensive survey of online expression issues in any one country or in the region as a whole. We hope to expand our information base and to keep it up-to-date, and welcome queries and comments sent to:

Human Rights Watch
Middle East and North Africa Division
1630 Connecticut Avenue, NW, Fifth Floor
Washington, DC 20009 USA
fax (202)612-4333
hrwdc@hrw.org

V. THE INTERNET IN THE MIDDLE EAST AND NORTH AFRICA: A CAUTIOUS START

The Middle East and North Africa is one of the most under-represented areas of the world in terms of per capita Internet connectivity. In a region where nearly every government censors or punishes speech critical of the authorities,[17] there can be little doubt that Internet growth has been slowed by the fear among those in power that democratizing Internet access will undermine state control over information. Saudi authorities stated bluntly during 1998 that the continuing delays in opening the Internet to public access were due to the search for a system by which authorities could block the flow of "undesirable" information.

But after a slow start, the spread of the Internet in the region has accelerated over the last four years. Pro-Internet forces within governments and in the business, academic, and research communities, wishing to keep current and globally competitive, have pushed for easier access to online data and communications.

As of May 1999, every country in the region except Iraq and Libya had some form of international connectivity. Members in all of these countries except Syria could connect to the Internet in some fashion via local Internet Service Providers (ISPs).[18]

At that time, there were an estimated 880,000 persons "online" in the Middle East, including Israel but excluding North Africa, according to Nua, a Dublin-based information technology firm (see table in Appendix A).[19] In at least fourteen countries (Morocco, Algeria, Tunisia, Egypt, Israel, the Palestinian self-rule areas,

---

[17] For country-by-country coverage of press restrictions, see the regularly updated reports of the Committee To Protect Journalists (<www.cpj.org/countrystatus>), Reporters sans Frontières (<www.rsf.fr>), Human Rights Watch (<www.hrw.org>), and the U.S. State Department's *Country Reports on Human Rights Practices* (<www.state.gov///www/global/human_rights/hrp_reports_mainhp.html>).

[18] An ISP is a company that provides Internet accounts, connections, and services to individuals and/or businesses.

[19] Nua's surveys, at <www.nua.ie/surveys/how_many_online>, are regularly updated. Its Middle East survey draws heavily on information collected by another company based in the United Arab Emirates, the Dabbagh Information Technology Group (<www.dit.net>). Nua cautions that the surveys are imprecise.

16

Lebanon, Jordan, Kuwait, Bahrain, Qatar, Iran, Oman, and the United Arab Emirates) cybercafés afforded the public access to the Internet for an hourly fee.[20]

The Arab press avidly follows Internet news, and conferences on the information revolution have become commonplace in the region. For example, Syria—which has yet to allow Internet access to the public—hosted the "Second Al-Shaam International Conference on Information Technology" in Damascus in April 1999.[21] Another indication of Internet growth is the publication in 1998 of a commercial yellow-pages, the *Middle East Internet Directory: A Comprehensive Guide to Middle East Web Sites* (<http://MiddleEastDirectory.com>).

The following examples demonstrate how the Internet is empowering citizens and nongovernmental forces, and eroding government-imposed controls on the flow of information:

- Through e-mail and web sites, human rights organizations in Egypt, the Palestinian territories, and elsewhere disseminate information far more effectively than ever before, despite their modest resources and limited access to the local media.[22]

- Arabic, English, and French newspapers that have been censored in Egypt, Algeria and Jordan have posted their banned stories online, where local and international readers can view them. Stories that newspapers declined to publish, due to political pressure or other factors, have circulated widely on the

---

[20] When visited on May 12, 1999, the web site <www.netcafeguide.com> provided a noncomprehensive list of fifty-three cybercafés in the Middle East and North Africa. For a profile of the first cybercafé to open in Iran, see Mike Theodoulou, "The Imams Are Wrestling with the Internet in the Battle for Nation's Young Minds," *The Times* (London), April 17, 1999, and Christophe de Roquefeuil, "Islam on line et croissants," *Libération*, December 10, 1998. On the first cybercafés in Algeria, see Cherif Ouazani, "Bab El Web City," *Jeune Afrique*, August 4, 1998. For a commentary by a Yemeni journalist decrying the absence of cybercafés in that country, see Walid al-Saqqaf, "How to Upgrade Use of the Internet," *Yemen Times*, February 1, 1999, <www.yementimes.com/99/iss05/techno.htm>.

[21] "Syrian Conference Calls for Wider Internet Access," Reuters, May 1, 1999.

[22] See Gallagher, "Middle East and North Africa Human Rights Activism in Cyberspace" and Deborah Wheeler, "In Praise of the Virtual Life: New Communications Technologies, Human Rights, Development, and the Defense of Middle Eastern Cultural Space" <www.cwrl.utexas.edu/~monitors/1.1/wheeler/index.html>. The web site on which this article appears is entitled *Monitors: A Journal of Human Rights and Technology.*

Internet.[23] When private dailies in Algeria went on strike in October 1998 to protest pressure from state-run printing presses, they published bulletins daily on the Web to mobilize support for their cause.[24] Internet-based organizations like the Digital Freedom Network (<www.dfn.org>) have been making censored materials available online. During 1998, the DFN posted articles that had been banned by authorities in Egypt, Mauritania, Tunisia, and Turkey.

- Citizens of Arab countries have debated and conversed with Israelis in "chat rooms" and other online forums at a time when it is difficult or impossible for them to have face-to-face contact, telephone conversations, and postal correspondence, due to travel restrictions and the absence of phone or mail links between most Arab countries and Israel.

- Moroccans can find copious information posted on the Web by the Polisario Front and others who challenge the official Moroccan line on the Western Sahara (see, for example, <www.arso.org>). Such information is either nonexistent or one-sided in the local news media, bookshops, and libraries.

---

[23] *Al-Quds Al-Arabi* was banned from entering Jordan on May 19, 1998. The London-based daily then took out advertisements in Jordanian newspapers directing readers to its online edition at <www.alquds.co.uk>. When Egyptian censors excised articles from the Nicosia-based *Middle East Times*, readers could view the censored material at the web site of the English-language weekly, <www.metimes.com>. In Algeria, journalists at the much-censored *La Nation* were able to post an edition of the weekly at the web site of Reporters sans Frontières, a French freedom of expression organization, after *La Nation* closed its doors in 1996 (<www.rsf.fr/censure/dazibao/index.html>).

[24] A writer at the Algiers-based French-language daily *El-Watan* wrote, "Sending out via the Internet special editions of the main private newspapers, which have been on strike for ten days, makes it possible to target a readership that follows what is happening in Algeria. Netsurfers, mostly Algerians who are dispersed throughout the world, can read in real time information that is addressed to them. This decision, made deliberately by editors who denounce the political pressures by the authorities, is a first. The World Wide Web is becoming indispensable. "La presse libre sur le web," October 27, 1998.

- Algerians can visit numerous web sites mounted by Islamist groups that are banned and have no legal publications inside Algeria, including the Front Islamique du Salut (<www. fisalgeria.org>).[25]

- An Arab Gay and Lesbian web site (<www.glas.org>) caters to people who, in many Arab countries, have few places to go to obtain information pertaining to their sexual orientation.

- The World Wide Web, with its online newspapers and radio and TV webcasting, has dramatically enhanced the diversity of news available to people in the Middle East. (So have the immensely popular Arabic-language satellite television stations.[26]) The change is especially marked for those living in countries where foreign newspapers are either unavailable, expensive, or out-of-date when they arrive.

Most countries that have allowed Internet access have tolerated freer expression online than is permitted in the local news media. Kuwait, Morocco, Algeria, Egypt, Jordan, and Lebanon have all permitted relatively unfettered online speech for the thousands of users in each country, even as they enforce press laws against print periodicals that publish "objectionable" material.

The extent of Internet connectivity in a country is determined by many factors in addition to government policies toward freedom of information and expression. These include the affordability to the public of computer equipment and of Internet and phone connections, and the state of a country's telecommunications

---

[25] On Algeria, see Christophe Labbé and Olivia Recasens, "Internet donne la parole aux Algériens," *Le Monde*, March 22, 1998.

[26] See Jon B. Altermann, *New Media, New Politics? From Satellite Television to the Internet in the Arab World* (Washington, DC: The Washington Institute for Near East Policy, 1998).

infrastructure, including such attributes as the number of telephone lines per capita[27] and the international connection's bandwidth.[28]

In most countries of the world that have known rapid Internet growth, the public sector has played a role by, among other things, building "backbone" telecommunications networks, providing initial funding, regulations, and standards, and by encouraging private investment and computer literacy. Thus, governments that favor development of the Internet must adopt affirmative policies, and not simply refrain from censorship and restricting access. Few governments in the Middle East and North Africa have embraced such an approach. The reasons include competing demands for scarce state resources, fear of losing control over information, and a desire to protect monopoly profits of state telecommunications companies.[29] Chakib Lahrichi, president of the independent Internet Association in Morocco, stated that while the Moroccan government had no explicit policy of censoring or restricting access to the Internet, its growth had been stunted by unfair advantages enjoyed by the state-controlled telecommunications company Itissalat

---

[27] For country-by-country statistics on telephones and computers, see The World Bank, *World Development Report: Knowledge for Development, 1998/99* (Oxford: Oxford University Press, published for the World Bank, 1999), pp. 226-227.

[28] Bandwidth is the amount of data that can flow over a network in a fixed amount of time. "Low bandwidth means slow, even excruciatingly slow, connections to the Internet which matter more with the more advanced uses such as the World Wide Web, especially under a unit-pricing regime [i.e., a slow bandwidth will require longer online time to perform the same tasks, thus hiking costs for users who pay for their phone service by time segments]. The Web is optimized for direct connection to the Internet such as through a university or corporate network. The more multimedia it becomes, with graphics, animation, sound, even video-conferencing, the greater its bandwidth demands. So the low bandwidth in Middle East local services and the high cost of international telephone calls charged by Middle Eastern telecommunication utilities discourage Web use, which is rarer in the region than e-mail and discussion groups." Jon Anderson, "The Internet and the Middle East: Commerce Brings Region On-Line," *Middle East Executive Reports*, vol. 20, no. 12, December 1997, </www.georgetown.edu/research/arabtech/meer97.htm>.

[29] On the often regressive role of telecommunication monopolies, see Muhammad Arif, "Al-mustaqbal li hatif al-Internet elethi yadkhal al-mantaqa al-'arabiyya bi-hathr," ("The future of Internet lines that are cautiously coming to the Arab world"), *al-Hayat* (London), July 8, 1998, and David Butter, "Telecoms Reform Takes the Lead," *Middle East Economic Digest*, May 8, 1998, pp. 2-3.

al-Maghrib in its competition with private service providers, along with the government's failure to educate the public about the Internet.[30]

The local prices of computer equipment or services also deter Internet use in many countries of the region. Those prices may reflect government attitudes toward popularizing Internet use, insofar as those prices are set, taxed or subsidized by the government. Throughout the region, Internet and telephone costs are more expensive than they are, for example, in the United States. They are even more costly when prevailing median income levels are taken into consideration.

Another factor inhibiting Internet growth in the region is the continuing dominance of English-language materials. Although the volume of material in Arabic is growing and the Arabic software available for browsing the Web is improving,[31] users who do not speak English remain at a disadvantage in their ability to access online resources.[32] French speakers, such as many North Africans, have access to significantly more materials than do monolingual Arabic speakers.

Some social forces have voiced hostility to the Internet or to its availability to the public at large. Legislators in Kuwait, Israel and elsewhere have denounced the Internet as a threat to local culture, morals, or religious sensibilities. In Iran, the clerical monthly *Sobh* called for a ban on the Internet.[33]

Governments and their supporters have sounded these themes to justify a go-slow, paternalistic approach to allowing public access to the Internet. For example, the spokesman of the Syrian Computer Society, which is chaired by the son of President Hafez al-Asad, was quoted as saying, "Our problem is...we are a

---

[30] Interview, Casablanca, April 30, 1998, and e-mail communication from Lahrichi to Human Rights Watch, May 12, 1999.

[31] The fact that, initially, much of the Arabic materials that were posted on the Web were posted as graphic files rather than as text files meant that they did not lend themselves to text searches, a key advantage of handling content online.

[32] Surveys of the presence of languages on the Web indicate that materials in English account for more than 80 percent of content, although that dominance seems to be declining. See, for example, "Web Languages Hit Parade," June 1997 (<http://babel.alis.com:8080/palmares.en.html>), compiled by the Babel Team, a joint initiative of Alis Technologies and the Internet Society. Arabic material accounts for only a tiny fraction of the remainder. See "Expert Calls for Promotion of Arabic on Internet," Xinhua news agency, December 30, 1998.

[33] Neil MacFarquhar, "With Mixed Feelings, Iran Tiptoes to the Internet," *The New York Times*, October 8, 1996.

traditional society and we have to know if there is something that cannot fit with our society. We have to make it safe."[34]

Similar arguments have been made by Saudis. Saleh Abdulrahman al-'Adhel, the head of the King Abdul-Aziz City for Science and Technology (KACST), reportedly stated that the Internet presents "an important service in relaying and distributing information but also has a negative side that conflicts with our faith and our Arab Muslim traditions."[35] The chair of the Saudi technology company Silkinet, explaining delays in allowing local Internet access, stated, "Efforts are ongoing to provide the best of modern technology, while ensuring that this does not conflict with the traditions and culture of the region."[36]

While sites of Western origin still dominate the Internet, many advocates of Islam and Islamism have embraced the Internet as a means of projecting their message. Of all the region's political opposition forces, Islamists are among the most active online, thanks partly to a large number of computer-literate activists living in Europe and North America. At an international meeting in July 1998 in Cairo, Islamic organizations and personalities vowed to use the new information technologies to enhance the image of Islam.[37] The Islamic Society of North America scheduled for May 1999 a conference devoted to using the Internet "as a tool for effective presentation of knowledge on Islam" (see <www.islamicinternet. org>). In Iran, an official announced in June 1998 that the complete works of the late Ayatollah Ruhollah Khomeini would soon be available online in various languages.[38] A computer institute in the city of Qom was preparing 2,000 Islamic instructional documents for presentation on the Web. The institute's director,

---

[34] Jack Redden, "Internet Arrives in Syria, But Not without Limits," Reuters, July 10, 1998. An e-mail sent by Human Rights Watch to the SCS seeking comment on the Reuters story went unanswered.

[35] Associated Press, May 12, 1997.

[36] "Leery Saudis Get Wired," Reuters, May 6, 1998.

[37] Muhammad Salah, "Al-Azhar wa al-Jama'at al-Islamiyya yatanafasan 'ala al-Internet," ("Al-Azhar and the Islamic Group compete on the Internet") *al-Hayat*, July 28, 1998. See also "Egypt's Moslem authorities to launch Islamic web site," Agence France-Presse, July 15, 1998.

[38] "Iran to put Khomeini's complete works on Internet," Agence France-Presse, June 1, 1998.

Sheikh Ali Korani, defended the Internet thus: "Many things have...a double nature and the Internet is one of them," he explained. "You can use it in different ways. The main thing is to use it for the good. And at present our clergy have not said that it is forbidden."[39]

No Middle East or North African government, not even the wariest, today wishes to be seen as anti-Internet. Syrian and Saudi officials assured their citizenry that the public would soon have access to the Internet, even as they invoked social conservatism to justify a gradual approach. The official *Tishrin* daily of January 27, 1997 reported that Internet subscriptions would be open to the Syrian public in six months, according to a dispatch the same day from United Press International. Twenty-eight months later, press reports from Syria continued to forecast that public Internet access would soon be available. In Saudi Arabia, *al-Jazira* newspaper reported on May 12, 1997 that King Fahd had agreed in principle to allow public access. It was not until January 1999 that local ISPs were allowed to serve ordinary citizens—almost five years after state institutions were first linked to the Internet. The long wait was necessary to "finalize the technology needed to bar access to information which is contrary to our Islamic values and dangerous to our security," explained the head of a group studying the issue at Riyadh's chamber of commerce and industry.[40]

Regulators around the world argue that curbs on freedom of expression on the Internet are needed to protect children from harmful content, preserve religious values, safeguard local cultures, protect national security, thwart terrorists, and silence racists. In the Middle East and North Africa, few officials will admit that blocking unwelcome political information is among their objectives in imposing controls on the Internet. In the Persian Gulf countries, note scholars Grey E. Burkhart and Seymour E. Goodman, pornography is "almost always first mentioned" when it comes to what the Internet "may do to national, cultural and religious values." Among other topics raised were "proselytizing by other religions and the availability of un-Islamic information (such as how to commit suicide), the potential effects on women's roles in society, [and] dilution of local cultural

---

[39] "Islam, Iran and the Internet," CNN Interactive (<www.cnn.com/WORLD/9705/22/iran.tech/index.html>), May 22, 1997.

[40] Habib Trabelsi, "Saudis Near End of Seven-Year Wait To Surf the Net," Agence France-Presse, July 15, 1998.

norms." These concerns, they write, surfaced "in the press and in our interviews with government, business, academic, religious and private individuals."[41]

Saudi Arabia has gone furthest in defining the scope of what kind of data it wished to keep off the Internet: its Council of Ministers issued a decree requiring service providers to refrain from "carrying out any activities violating the social, cultural, political, media, economic, and religious values of the Kingdom of Saudi Arabia."[42]

U.A.E. officials told Human Rights Watch that keeping out pornography was the only objective of the U.A.E.'s Internet censorship regime. Officials of other countries and corporate representatives of ISPs in the region have spoken more generally of protecting cultural values. For example, a representative of Teleyemen, Yemen's monopoly ISP, told Human Rights that the Teleyemen was under "a general requirement" to "limit access to information which is considered to be undesirable in terms of causing offence against social, religious, or cultural standards." Like the U.A.E. and Saudi Arabia, Yemen filters what users can access through the use of a proxy server and "censorware."[43] A proxy server is a device that is interposed between users and the Internet; in response to user requests and according to the criteria it is programmed to follow, the proxy examines material requested by a user and either delivers it or blocks its delivery.

Pro-Active Approaches by Governments

Governments have responded to the advent of the Internet pro-actively as well as by censorship and regulation. Every Middle East government has launched one or more web sites to get its voice heard amidst the din of alternative information sources in cyberspace.[44] Saudi Arabia, Bahrain, Egypt, Iran, Israel, Kuwait,

---

[41] Grey E. Burkhart and Seymour E. Goodman, "The Internet Gains Acceptance in the Persian Gulf," *Communications of the ACM*, March 1998, vol. 41 no.3. The ACM is the Association for Computing Machinery.

[42] Quoted in *Al-Jazira* newspaper, May 6, 1998, as reported in Foreign Broadcast Information Service, Near East and South Asia (hereafter FBIS), May 12, 1998.

[43] Letter to Human Rights Watch from Christopher D. Leather, Teleyemen Divisional Manager, August 8, 1998. The letter is reprinted in Appendix C of this report.

[44] Directories of government sites can be found at <www.gksoft.com/govt> and <www.agora.stm.it/politic>. A brief overview is provided in Jonathan B. Lincoln, "Middle East Governments on the World Wide Web," *WINEP Research Notes*, no. 6 (Washington,

Morocco, Oman, Tunisia and the Palestinian Authority are among those that webcast state radio and/or television.

Saudi Arabia has invested heavily in getting its message out, through an Internet presence (see, for example, the official site <www.saudi.net>) and also through ownership by pro-government Saudis of influential Europe-based Arab newspapers, magazines, and broadcast media. One apparent impetus has been a wish to counter small London-based Saudi dissident groups, such as the Committee for the Defense of Legitimate Rights (<www.ummah.org.uk/cdlr>) and the Movement for Islamic Reform in Arabia (<www.miraserve.com>), which had achieved a high profile through adroit use of fax machines and the Internet.[45]

The government of Tunisia maintains several sites containing official information and links to pro-government media (see, e.g., <www.tunisiaonline.com>). Its public relations efforts were aided by a pro-Tunisian businessman in Paris who launched a web site that had an appearance likely to fool viewers into thinking they had accessed an Amnesty International web site about Tunisia. The site, <www.amnesty-tunisia.org> offered only favorable information about Tunisia's human rights record and nothing related to the findings of Amnesty International.[46]

Numerous articles in the regional press have urged a more active "Arab" presence on the Internet. An article in the official Damascus daily *Tishrin*, deploring the fact that Web-based resources dealing with the Arab-Israeli conflict were dominated by materials of Israeli origin, called for "check[ing] all that is placed on the Internet on Syria and confront[ing] it by giving explanations or correcting distorted information."[47] The Syrian Arab News Agency launched a web site in 1998 (<www.sana.org>) to propagate official news and viewpoints at a time when local Internet access was unavailable to the Syrian public.

DC: Washington Institute for Near East Policy, February 1999).

[45] The strongest manifestation of official displeasure with the dissident groups came in 1995, when the Saudis threatened Great Britain with a cutoff of defense contracts if CDLR spokesman Muhammad Mas'ari was not somehow silenced. The British government attempted to deport Mas'ari but was thwarted by Britain's courts.

[46] The businessman denied that the use of "amnesty" in the web site address was intended to fool users. See Country Profiles, below.

[47] Husayn al-Ibrahim, "The Internet and Informatics [sic] in the Arab-Israeli Conflict," *Tishrin*, February 23, 1998, as reported in FBIS, March 1, 1998.

In a few countries, national and local governments are using the Internet to make it easier for citizens to consult official information and communicate with authorities. Several of Jordan's government ministries, as well as the General Intelligence Services (<www.nic.gov.jo/gid>), maintain their own sites and invite e-mail correspondence. Morocco (<www.mincom.gov.ma>), Egypt (via <www.mfa.gov.eg>, the Foreign Ministry site), and the Palestinian Authority (<www.pna.net>) have taken steps in this direction. However, few Arab governments have embarked on a systematic effort to put online information that would enhance informed political participation by their publics—materials such as legal and regulatory codes, draft legislation, official reports and statistics, transcripts of press conferences and parliamentary debates, court rulings, and economic data used to define budget allocations.

VI. CYBERCENSORSHIP: ITS VARIOUS FORMS

The Internet offers protean possibilities for evading controls on the flow of information. In countries where there is no local ISP, persons can, for the price of an international call, dial service providers in other countries. If a web site is blocked, its sponsors or fans can change its address or "mirror" the same content at other World Wide Web sites. Local users can view web sites that are blocked by accessing them via free "anti-censorship proxy (ACP) servers." [48] They can also have persons who enjoy access to content that is blocked locally e-mail it to them as attached files. Wary e-mail correspondents can foil surveillance by using pseudonymous e-mail accounts or encryption, or by routing messages through a Web-based re-mailing service that "anonymizes" them by stripping information that identifies the sender.

But if the tricks available to users are bountiful, so is the technology on the other side of the cat-and-mouse game. Governments may not be able to stop, but they can certainly slow the flow of "objectionable" content and thus buy time to adjust to an era in which their ability to block or crowd out information is diminished.

State's can deny the public local access to the Internet altogether, as Iraq, Libya, Syria and, until recently Saudi Arabia have done. But neither Syria nor Saudi Arabia has gone so far as to prohibit possession of modems or connections to foreign Internet providers. Both Riyadh and Damascus have thus tolerated a limited and gradually increasing amount of Internet access rather than adopt the

---

[48] Brian Ristuccia, an American who set up a free, web-based anti-censorship proxy (ACP) server, <www.osiris.ml.org>, explained that his ACP works by creating an alternate namespace for the entire Internet. "This means that every site on the entire Internet is made to appear as if it is a page on my server....The ACP server is a very effective Internet censorship repair tool because it takes only one unblocked site to unblock the entire Internet." He warned, however, that if surveillance is being conducted of Internet users, their activities via the ACP server are not protected from monitoring. He said in March 1999 that the latest version of his ACP "makes it more difficult for proxy administrators to see what sites a person has viewed, because each URL is assigned a random time-expired token that only the proxy server knows the actual value for."

The Osiris ACP received heavy traffic from users in the United Arab Emirates, among other countries, Ristuccia said, but was being blocked by the Saudi authorities. E-mail communication from Brian Ristuccia to Human Rights Watch, January 7, 1999 and March 11, 1999.

draconian measures required to prevent access to foreign ISPs, which would likely antagonize the members of the public wealthy enough to afford it.

Governments that presently allow public local access to the Internet have adopted a range of methods to regulate that access. The Global Internet Liberty Campaign divides these methods into four categories: Internet-specific laws; application of existing laws; content-based license (or contract) terms applied to users and service providers, and compulsory use of filtering, rating or content labeling tools.[49] All of these methods can be found in the Middle East and North Africa, along with extra-legal measures that also diminish online freedoms.

Laws and licensing terms. Tunisia has developed the region's most detailed Internet-specific laws. Tunisia also explicitly extends to the Internet existing press laws limiting free expression, something that few other countries in the region have done. However, the existing press laws of several countries, in their delineation of offenses, define "publishing" or "disseminating" information in so broad a fashion that no new laws are needed to bring Internet speech under their purview. Qatari Internet users must sign a contract with the Qatar Public Telecommunications Corporation (Q.Tel) pledging not to use the service to "carry out any activity which is contrary to public order" (article 3.2.4). Asked for the definition of this phrase, Qatar's embassy in Washington replied that while there is no "concise definite context of the phrase," it "refers in general to the necessity of commitment to the State's public policies and to the community's traditions and values."[50]

Filtering of content. The United Arab Emirates has set up a "proxy server" that denies user access to sites deemed inappropriate, mostly because of their explicit sexuality. Bahrain, Iran, Yemen, Tunisia, and Saudi Arabia also block web sites, using a variety of technical means available to filter and block content. Blocking is easier to implement for governments that retain control over the national telecommunications network, including the international gateways. Nearly everywhere in the region, telecommunications remain a state-controlled monopoly. And even in the few countries that have allowed some privatization of Internet services, such as Egypt, the international gateway remains under state control.

In addition to technical and legal means, other government practices, including threats and intimidation, can create a chilling effect on online speech, just as such practices often do more than press laws to constrain what private newspapers and

---

[49] Global Internet Liberty Campaign, *Regardless of Frontiers,* pp. 11-12.

[50] Undated written communication to Human Rights Watch, received November 1998 and reprinted in Appendix C.

magazines are willing to print. Fears of government surveillance or reprisals, for example, can foster self-censorship in a newspaper, a web site, or an online "chat room." In Jordan, for example, at least two persons were reportedly summoned for questioning by the police during 1996 because of articles or comments they had posted on electronic bulletin boards or in chat rooms—forums whose contents can be read by everyone, including the police (see section on Jordan, below).

No government in the region, to our knowledge, has admitted to "eavesdropping" on e-mail, and Human Rights Watch has no proof that it is taking place. Yet given the technical ease of conducting this sort of surveillance—especially when all Internet access goes through a gateway that is maintained by a state-controlled institution— and the fact that police forces in so many countries of the region tap the phones and open the mail of real and suspected dissidents, it is not surprising to hear fears expressed by Internet users in Tunisia, Bahrain, and other countries about the privacy of their electronic communications. Authorities monitor telephone conversations in at least thirteen countries of the region, according to the U.S. Department of State's *Country Reports on Human Rights Practices* for 1998, and in most they did so without legally issued warrants or judicial supervision. Those who suspect online surveillance often cite instances of e-mails inexplicably disappearing en route or taking two days to reach their destination. Such occurrences can be caused by snooping but of course may have other explanations as well.

Governments have also pursued old-fashioned forms of surveillance against online expression. In March 1997 Bahraini authorities detained a telecommunications engineer suspected of transmitting information to opposition groups abroad via his computer, which was confiscated. According to sources abroad, the engineer, Sayyid 'Alawi Sayyid Sharaf, came under suspicion not through high-tech surveillance but through the traditional methods of the secret police, including the interrogation of third parties and the use of informants (see section on Bahrain, below).

VII. GOVERNMENT-IMPOSED FILTERING SCHEMES VIOLATE THE RIGHT TO FREE EXPRESSION

Government-imposed filtering poses two basic threats to the right to free expression. First, as explained in the legal section above, it constitutes a form of prior censorship and as such should be subjected to the strictest level of scrutiny. Second, in practical terms, the filtering technologies developed so far are imprecise tools. Even when the stated motives for content-filtering have been justifiable, such as to keep pornographic materials from minors,[51] the means used have almost invariably impeded, whether intentionally or not, the flow of political, cultural, medical and other types of content that are unquestionably legal under international standards.

In Bahrain, Iran, Saudi Arabia, the United Arab Emirates, and Yemen, ISPs—either under government orders or pressure—all block web sites on the basis of their content.[52] In the first four if not all of these countries, blocking extends to cultural and/or political content.

U.A.E. officials are perhaps more forthcoming than others that engage in blocking. They justify it as a means of limiting access to pornography. Persons in the Emirates who dial up a local service provider do not have unmediated access to the Internet. Rather, their requests are routed through a proxy server maintained by the government-controlled telecommunications company, Etisalat.[53] When a user requests a web site, the request will be refused if the filtering software on the proxy server detects "objectionable" material on the site or finds that the site is on a list of banned sites. The presence on the U.A.E.'s list of taboo sites of a political and cultural web site for Arab homosexuals refutes official claims that only pornography is banned (see below).

---

[51] The International Covenant on Civil and Political Rights permits, in article 19, restrictions on speech "for the protection of...public health or morals"—but only "such as are provided by law and are necessary."

[52] It is often difficult to confirm which web sites are being blocked by a government and for what duration. The inaccessibility of a site may have other causes such as a surge in demand or technical glitches. Also, governments generally do not comment on which web sites they block, and sites sometimes are blocked only intermittently.

[53] Users can circumvent the U.A.E.'s proxy server if they dial into an ISP in another country, or if they can access an anti-censorship proxy server.

A proxy server such as the ones in place in the U.A.E. and Saudi Arabia can be used by authorities to track which computer terminals are accessing which web sites and for how long. U.A.E. authorities deny monitoring individual web use. In Saudi Arabia, however, users who request a site that is blocked get a message on their screens warning that all access attempts are logged.[54]

State-controlled or state-influenced Internet Service Providers in Tunisia, Iran, and Bahrain block web sites containing political or human rights criticism of the government. Tunisia has acknowledged blocking only those sites that offend moral values, but apparently this includes the sites of various human rights organizations critical of the government (see below).

Bahrain has been less aggressive than neighboring Saudi Arabia and the U.A.E. in trying to block pornography centrally. Although there are reports that it is blocking some sexually explicit sites, Batelco, the state-controlled monopoly service provider, seems to rely more on encouraging subscribers to download filtering programs, should they desire it.

The ability of minors to access online pornography was one impetus for the enactment in 1996 by the U.S. Congress of the Communications Decency Act (CDA). The act criminalized online communication that is "obscene, lewd, lascivious, filthy, or indecent, with intent to annoy, abuse, threaten, or harass another person," or "obscene or indecent" if the recipient of the communication is under eighteen years of age.

The CDA was opposed by a coalition of human rights and free expression groups. As Human Rights Watch, a member group of the coalition, argued in an affidavit to the Supreme Court, the law's prohibition of "indecent" speech could be applied to its own human rights reporting that includes graphic accounts of rape and other forms of sexual abuse. In an important ruling for Internet liberties, the U.S. Supreme Court in 1997 voided key provisions of the act on the grounds that the Internet is entitled to the highest level of free speech protection and the act violated that principle.[55]

While cautioning that all methods of controlling access to Internet content pose dangers to the right to impart and receive information, some international civil

---

[54] Douglas Jehl, "The Internet's 'Open Sesame' Is Answered Warily," *New York Times*, March 18, 1999.

[55] *Reno v. American Civil Liberties Union*, 117 S. Ct. 2329, 138 L.Ed.2d. 874 (1997).

liberties organizations have argued that filtering software installed by the end-user raises fewer freedom-of-speech concerns than censorship imposed from above.[56]

Filtering software works by examining a data stream and blocking any material that matches specified criteria, such as the presence of "stop words" in a web site's home page or URL, or the presence of the URL on a list of banned sites A more aggressive type of software, such as the KidDesk Internet Safe program, "white-lists" material by prohibiting access to *all* materials *except* those that are explicitly approved by the parent or supervisor.

Making the case that end-user filtering software is a "lesser evil," the Center for Democracy and Technology, a Washington, D.C.-based organization, argues:

> By placing control over content in the hands of individual parents, as opposed to bureaucrats and prosecutors, policy makers can assure full respect for our constitutional protection of freedom of expression and enable the Internet to grow free from unnecessary and ineffective regulatory interference....A great variety of blocking and filtering software exists which can serve the diversity of family values of American communities, providing choice to families online without infringing the constitutional First Amendment rights of Internet users.[57]

---

[56] For a brief account of the pros and cons of various methods of regulating access by minors to sexually explicit material online, see Joseph Westfall, "Cybersmut," *Issues in Ethics,* vol. 9 (Winter 1998), pp. 6-10; reprinted in *Business and Society Review*, no.102/103 (1998), pp. 89-94.

[57] "Internet Family Empowerment White Paper: How Filtering Tools Enable Responsible Parents to Protect Their Children Online," A White Paper prepared by the Center for Democracy and Technology, July 16, 1997, <www.cdt.org/speech/summary.html>. The American Civil Liberties Union writes, "While user-based blocking programs present troubling free speech concerns, we still believe today that they are far preferable to any statute that imposes criminal penalties on online speech. In contrast, many of the new ratings schemes [systems in which content is rated according to certain criteria and inappropriate material is then blocked] pose far greater free speech concerns than do user-based software programs." "Fahrenheit 451.2: Is Cyberspace Burning? How Rating and Blocking Proposals May Torch Free Speech on the Internet," American Civil Liberties Union, August 7, 1997, <www.aclu.org/issues/cyber/burning.html>. See also, Cyber-Rights and Cyber-Liberties (UK), "Who Watches the Watchmen: Internet Content Rating Systems and Privatised Censorship," November 1997, <www.cyber-rights.org/watchmen.htm>.

Whether employed by end-users or government servers, filtering software is an imprecise tool that in practice almost always blocks materials beyond its stated purpose. This is true even of the more sophisticated products that are regularly updated by staff members who check web sites for "su tability."[58] According to popular anecdotes, software that hunted for specified "stop words" ended up blocking sites that mentioned the English county of Middlesex and recipes for chicken breasts. One popular program blocked a web site containing information on AIDS prevention. Even a pro-filtering web site was once blocked by Surf Watch, a leading filtering program, because it shared a commercial server with a pornographic site.[59]

---

[58] See Electronic Privacy Information Center, "Faulty Filters: How Content Filters Block Access to Kid-Friendly Information on the Internet," December 1997, <www2.epic.org/reports/filter-report.html>. A bibliography of reports and articles critical of filtering software is posted on the web site of the Internet Free Expression Alliance, <www.ifea.net>. See also the "Censorship - Academic & Educational - Library Filtering" Archive on the web site of the Electronic Freedom Foundation (<www.eff.org>). The latter contains "Kids and the Internet: The Promises and the Perils," a December 1998 paper by member organizations of the Internet Free Expression Alliance which critiques filtering software and discusses alternatives.

[59] Matt Richtel, "Tables Turn on a Filtering Site As It Is Temporarily Blocked," *New York Times*, March 11, 1999.

VIII. CONTENT AND CARRIER: THE QUESTION OF LIABILITY

The development of the Internet has spurred the promulgation of new laws, as well as the often-hasty application to the Internet of existing media laws. One controversy that has flared in several countries is over apportioning liability for objectionable content that appears online.[60] Is an Internet Service Provider that hosts a web site or "chat room" responsible for its content, or is the originator of the offending content (for example, the author) solely responsible? And should a cybercafé be responsible for messages sent by clients from its premises?

As noted above, the right to free expression is best served by laws that focus liability on the originator of the offending content, rather than on its conduit. But at least one country in the region, Tunisia, has promulgated laws holding ISPs liable for content, including statutes requiring the ISP director to "maintain constant oversight of the content of the ISP's servers to insure that no information remains on the system that is contrary to public order and good morals."

The European Commission, in a 1996 report, stated, "Internet access providers and host service providers play a key role in giving users access to Internet content. It should not however be forgotten that the prime responsibility for content lies with authors and content providers." ISPs "should not be targeted by the individual governments and law enforcement bodies where the ISPs have no control of the Internet content."[61] This approach was endorsed by the European Parliament on May 13, 1998 and by the Council of the European Union in a "recommendation" formally adopted on September 24, 1998.[62]

In the U.S., the Communications Decency Act of 1996 clearly distinguishes, for the purpose of assigning liability, the content provider from those who transmit

---

[60] See <www.gilc.org/speech/liability> for information about ISP liability jurisprudence in several Western countries.

[61] <www2.echo.lu/legal/en/Internet/communic.html>.

[62] "Council Recommendation of 24 September 1998 on the development of the competitiveness of the European audiovisual and information services industry by promoting national frameworks aimed at achieving a comparable and effective level of protection of minors and human dignity," <http://europa.eu.int/comm/dg10/avpolicy/new_srv/recom-intro_en.html>. For more on European Union policy toward the Internet, see Penny Campbell and Emmanuelle Machet, "European Policy on Regulation of Content on the Internet," in the National Council for Civil Liberties, ed., *Liberating Cyberspace: Civil Liberties, Human Rights and the Internet* (London: Pluto Press, 1999), pp. 140-158.

the content. The CDA's section 230(c)(1), amending the Communications Act of 1934, states, "[No] provider or user of an interactive computer service shall be treated as the publisher or speaker of any information provided by another information content provider." Several European countries have adopted or proposed legislation limiting the liability of access providers for content provided by third parties.[63]

Cybercafés are shops where persons can walk in off the street and use Internet-connected computers for a fee. Among their patrons are persons who have no other means of accessing the Internet, as well as persons who seek a measure of anonymity or privacy they feel they do not have when using their own computers.

The fluid nature of the clientele of cybercafés has aroused concerns among some governments. In Vietnam, security officials shut down a cybercafé after expressing objections to e-mails that were allegedly sent from it.[64] In Singapore, which has legislation regulating content on the Internet and imposing oversight responsibility on ISPs, an anonymous comment in February 1996 sent from a cybercafé to the <soc.culture.singapore> newsgroup immediately resulted in an apology from the cafe's owners and a disassociation from the content of the posting. Apparently fearing government pressures, several Singaporean cybercafés then reportedly reconfigured their equipment so that patrons could browse but no longer post material in newsgroups.[65] In Tunisia, at least some Internet cafés pursue practices that limit user privacy and anonymity, according to a European journalist who visited two locations in greater Tunis in February 1999. The terminals in both shops were arranged so that all of the monitor screens were visible from a single point in the room. In one location, clients were required to present identity documents to the staff; in the other they were required to provide their names and addresses.

---

[63] For example, Germany's Information and Communications Services Act, article 1 section 5, states, "[Internet Service] Providers shall not be responsible for any third-party content which they make available for use unless they have knowledge of such content and are technically able and can reasonably be expected to block the use of such content." But this legislation does not fully allay free-speech concerns about the burden placed on the ISP.

[64] David Case, "Big Brother Is Alive and Well in Vietnam—And He Really Hates the Web," *Wired*, vol. 5, no.11 (November 1997) .

[65] Gary Rodan, "The Internet and Political Control in Singapore," *Political Science Quarterly*, vol. 113, no. 1, Spring 1998, pp. 63-90, <http://epn.org/psq/rodan.html> or <http://tap.epn.org/psq/rodan.html>.

IX. HOW USERS CAN PROTECT THEIR RIGHTS
TO PRIVACY AND ANONYMITY

Internet communication is highly vulnerable to surveillance and interception. A government agency can violate the privacy of e-mail correspondence just as easily as it can tap a person's telephone in order to listen to conversations or intercept faxes. The equipment needed is neither costly nor complicated to operate.

Authorities can monitor by tapping an individual phone line and intercepting data streams as they are sent and received. If a user has Internet access via a private ISP, employees of that ISP can open and read e-mail sent through it or allow police investigators to do so, unless special safeguards are put in place to protect privacy. If authorities have access to an ISP's server or the country's telecommunications network, they can capture e-mails while they are in transit.

Authorities can read, block, or delete messages based on such criteria as the e-mail address of the sender or the recipient, the Internet Protocol addresses identifying the sending computer and the destination computer(s), or the presence of specified character strings in the body of the message—say, the words "Emir" and "corruption" in close proximity. Such a system is analogous to a postal delivery system in which all pieces of mail are first delivered to a single location, where officials can inspect items at will.

Although data is broken up and sent in "packets," each packet contains Internet Protocol (IP) addresses. Packets can easily be reassembled while en route with the aid of eavesdropping tools.

An eavesdropper can generally identify the computer terminal that is sending or receiving data, but not the person who is typing on its keyboard. For this reason, some governments are uneasy about allowing computer terminals with Internet access in places where extra effort would be required to monitor who is using each terminal, for what, and when. A contract provided by Tunisia's state-run Agence Tunisienne d'Internet (ATI) requires institutional Internet subscribers to refrain from offering anyone remote access via their computers without prior authorization, and to declare to the ATI the names of all persons having accounts on, or access to, the computers and to inform the agency of changes in the user list.

Expression via the Internet includes the use of means that are private and others that are public. E-mail is private in the sense that the sender specifies the persons and addresses to whom it will be sent. (Of course, recipients can then re-send it to others or post it on a bulletin board, just as they can do with an ordinary letter.) By contrast, launching an open-access web site or posting a comment in a public newsgroup are acts of public speech since they are viewable by anyone who wishes to visit the web site or newsgroup.

Computer users have various means to protect their privacy and anonymity, some more effective than others. At the low-tech end, a user can try to avoid surveillance by using a computer terminal or e-mail account that is not being monitored, for example, one belonging to a friend. The user can dial into another country and bypass the local service provider or use a pseudonymous e-mail account from one of the many companies that offer web-based e-mail accounts and that do not require clients to furnish their real names, such as MSN.com's "Hotmail," Yahoo.com's "Yahoo! mail," and USA.net's "Web@ddress." These techniques may help users escape identification if they are not already under surveillance, but they are no insurance against interception if a user's computer communication is being monitored.[66]

Experts agree that there are basically three methods that, for the time being at least, make surveillance extremely difficult: direct-to-satellite and other forms of wireless transmission, anonymous re-mailers, and encryption.

Small dishes are available that enable users to transmit and receive data directly via satellite, bypassing the ground-based telecommunication system. These fit into a suitcase-sized carrying case and can be placed discreetly on a balcony while in use. They resemble in size the "pizza" dishes used to download satellite television broadcasts, but are capable of sending as well as receiving. Some countries of the Middle East and North Africa either ban or require permits for direct-to-satellite dishes. Cost also puts this technology beyond the reach of most individuals and nongovernmental organizations in the region. But as they grow more affordable and widespread, wireless communications offer a potent means of evading government monitoring and censorship.

Encryption, on the other hand, costs nothing or next to nothing. Strong and easy-to-use encryption software, such as the "Pretty Good Privacy" (PGP) program, can be downloaded for free from the World Wide Web and stored on a laptop or personal computer.[67] While experts using powerful computers have been able to

---

[66] Most web-based free e-mail services are not encrypted. Users could enhance security when using these services by encrypting and/or anonymizing the messages they send. See below.

[67] See Patrick Ball and Mark Girouard, *Safe Communications in a Dangerous World: Cryptographic Applications for Human Rights Groups* (Washington, DC: American Association for the Advancement of Science, expected 1999). For information about how PGP, a "public key" encryption program, works, see the FAQ (frequently asked questions)

break strong encryption codes, the process requires considerable resources and time and is impractical for routine monitoring. Users should nevertheless pay attention to developments in the field—as well as to local laws governing the use of encryption. The Global Internet Liberty Campaign maintains a country-by-country review of legislation at <www.gilc.org/crypto/crypto-survey.html# country>.

The right to encrypt messages is of particular importance to the protection of human rights. In many countries human rights organizations use PGP to protect the identity of witnesses and victims when sending data electronically. Rights groups in Guatemala, Ethiopia, Haiti, Mexico, South Africa, Hong Kong, and Turkey are among those that use encryption, according the GILC survey. Some groups use cryptographic techniques to digitally sign messages that they send over the Internet to ensure their integrity and authenticity, that is, to prove the messages are indeed coming from them and have not been altered in transmission.

The power of encryption to foil monitoring has led a number of governments to impose restrictions on the use, sale, and export of encryption software. Tunisia, Saudi Arabia, and Israel are among those countries that ban the use of encryption without prior authorization.[68]

Encryption has an Achilles heel: it may effectively shield a message's contents from an eavesdropper but not the fact that something has been encoded. This alone may lead to harsh consequences if the authorities wish to punish the sender or recipient, or coerce them to disclose the message's contents or their "private keys." Upon obtaining the latter, authorities could then read every message encrypted with the user's "public key" or use the compromised private key to impersonate that user in corresponding with others.

One way to circumvent this danger is to camouflage encrypted messages by using steganography. This type of program hides one form of data inside another—for example, text inside a graphic image or a video or audio clip—in such

---

sheets at <http://www.arc.unm.edu/~drosoff/pgp/pgp.html> and <www.cam.ac.uk.pgp.net/ pgpnet/pgp-faq>; see also David Banisar, *BUG OFF! A Primer for Human Rights Groups on Wiretapping* (London: Privacy International, October 1995), <www.privacy.org/pi/ reports/bug_off.html>.

[68] According to GILC's encryption survey, other countries with laws restricting encryption include Belarus, Singapore, Russia, Pakistan, China, and until January 1999, France. In the United States, encrypting is not regulated, but laws bar U.S. companies from freely exporting strong encryption software without a license, on the grounds that encryption will be used by terrorists, drug traffickers, and organized crime groups to conceal their deeds.

a way that makes it more likely to escape detection by interlopers. For example, a sensitive document proving that a police unit moonlighted as a death squad can be encrypted and embedded in a photograph of a soccer team, and then e-mailed to a person outside the country who has the means to extract the document. Steganography software can be downloaded for free from the World Wide Web.[69] However, some experts warn that sophisticated eavesdroppers can detect when a file has something steganographically hidden in it.

The third anti-surveillance strategy is to route communications via secure and trusted web-based re-mailing services that forward them to the designated recipient only after expunging the original address and other identifying data.[70] To reduce traceability further, users can select re-mailers that keep no records of the addresses from which they receive, and to which they send, data. They can also program messages to pass through more than one re-mailer; some re-mailers do this automatically. And if their browser supports strong encryption, they can choose a re-mailer that encrypts all messages as they are sent to that re-mailer, which then sends them on to the intended recipient in decrypted form. In the latter scenario, even if an eavesdropper is "sniffing" a person's Internet activities, the eavesdropper can at most discern that the person is visiting a particular web site but not the content of the messages that the person is sending, the intended recipients, or whether the person has encrypted messages before sending them.

For obvious reasons, some governments see anonymizing re-mailers as undesirable and have blocked them.[71] The governments of China, Singapore, and the United Arab Emirates block the web site of www.anonymizer.com, one of the best-known such services, according to Lance Cottrell, president of

---

[69] For more on steganography, see <http://members.iquest.net/~mrmil/stego.html>.

[70] Useful information about anonymous re-mailers can be found in the Anonymous Re-mailer FAQ (frequently asked questions) by André Bacard, <www.well.com/user/abacard/remail.html>. See also <www.anonymizer.com>, which offers anonymizing re-mailer and web-browser services, a FAQ, and links to other sites that deal with privacy on the World Wide Web. For a list of active anonymizing re-mailers, see <www.cs.berkeley.edu/~raph/remailer-list.html>.

[71] On concerns in the law-enforcement community about anonymity on the Internet, see Steve Lohr, "Privacy on Internet Poses Legal Puzzle," *New York Times*, April 19, 1999.

Anonymizer.com.[72] Another potential problem with anonymizers is that they do not guarantee that the user's identity will remain unknown to the anonymizing service itself or to the user's ISP. Researcher are addressing this concern. One tool that is still in prototype form is "Crowds." It works by collecting Web users into a geographically diverse group that performs Web transactions on behalf of its individual members in a way that prevents Web servers, other "crowd" members, and eavesdroppers from identifying the sender of a particular communication.[73]

---

[72] Lance Cottrell, "Commercial Anonymity," paper presented at the Computers, Freedom and Privacy conference in Washington, DC on April 6, 1999, <www.cfp99.org/program/papers/cottrell.htm>.

[73] "Crowds" and other new tools for protecting privacy online are described in *Communications of the ACM*, February 1999 (vol. 42, no. 2). The ACM is the Association for Computing Machinery.

X. COUNTRY PROFILES

This section profiles the state of online liberties in eight countries of the Middle East and North Africa. The type of information it contains varies from country to country, and is not comprehensive. The length of each chapter entry is not necessarily indicative of the extent of Internet control or regulation in that country.

Bahrain

The Internet is the arena of two conflicting objectives of the Bahraini government: its bid to become "the telecommunications hub of the Gulf"[74] and its determination to suppress information critical of the rule of the Al Khalifa family. Authorities have on the one hand promoted the Internet, making access available since 1995 and easy to obtain. No authorization is required to launch a web site. Several Internet cafés serve the public. On the other hand, the security services are aware that the Bahraini opposition has skillfully used the Internet to collect and disseminate information. They have blocked web sites and reportedly employ technical experts to assist in conducting surveillance of Internet use.

According to one Bahraini professor who was interviewed in February 1999 and requested anonymity, "the situation of the Internet is good, better than the overall human rights situation, because the government understands its importance for maintaining a competitive business edge, especially in a service economy."

Bahrain's constitution guarantees freedom of speech, of the press, printing and publication, "in accordance with the conditions and procedure specified by the law." It also guarantees privacy of postal, telegraphic and telephonic communications. Article 26 states, "No communications shall be censored nor the contents thereof revealed except in cases of necessity prescribed by the law and in accordance with the procedures and guarantees stated therein."

Despite these constitutional provisions, authorities exercise sweeping control over all local media and make public criticism of government officials and policies off-limits. According to the U.S. State Department's *Country Reports on Human Rights Practices* for 1998, "Telephone calls and correspondence are subject to monitoring. Police informer networks are extensive and sophisticated. During the

---

[74] See, for example, "Bahrain: The Powerhouse of the Gulf," an eight-page advertising supplement in the December 21, 1998 issue of *Newsweek* magazine, U.S. edition.

year, the Government frequently infringed on citizens' right to privacy, using illegal searches and arbitrary arrests as tactics to control political unrest....E-mail access to information is unimpeded, although it may be subject to monitoring."

Bahraini authorities did not respond to Human Rights Watch's letter and follow-up inquiries requesting information on Internet policies. Internet service is a monopoly of the public telecommunications company Batelco. Prices are moderate but can add up since there is no option for unlimited service at a fixed price.

There are conflicting reports on the extent to which authorities block politically sensitive web sites. However, various sources concur that the web site of the Bahraini Freedom Movement (<http://ourworld.compuserve.com\homepages\bahrain>)—or at least the content beyond its home page—is systematically blocked. Unlike the United Arab Emirates and Saudi Arabia, Bahrain does not appear to have implemented an ambitious system to block pornography. It has preferred to encourage users concerned about sexually explicit materials to install filtering software.

Authorities are less concerned with blocking web sites than with closing down the sources of critical information leaking out of the country, according to the professor cited above. A small number of Bahrainis have reportedly been detained or questioned on suspicion of using electronic means to transmit information to political opposition groups outside the country. The best known case is that of Sayyid 'Alawi Sayyid Sharaf, a Batelco engineer. On the night of March 25, 1997 security forces raided Sharaf's home, confiscated his computer and detained him. He was held for nearly two years before being released without charge. According to a Bahraini who met Sharaf after his release, he came under suspicion not through high-tech means of surveillance but through the traditional police methods, including the interrogation of third parties and the use of informants. Amnesty International stated that Sharaf had reportedly been tortured while being held incommunicado by intelligence officials.[75]

Iraq

Iraq is the only country in West Asia that has no Internet connection at all. In a letter to Human Rights Watch, Iraq's Ambassador to the United Nations Nizar Hamdoon blamed this state of affairs on damage to the telecommunications

---

[75] Amnesty International Urgent Action Appeal 42/97, March 25, 1997.

infrastructure inflicted during the Gulf War and to the U.N. sanctions[76] that restrict imports of spare parts for this sector. He suggested that but for these foreign obstacles, the government of Iraq would be pursuing a pro-Internet policy. In his letter, the ambassador affirmed that Iraq's constitutional guarantees of freedom of opinion encompass the right to receive and disseminate information online, "in conformity with the aims of the constitution and within the limits of the Law." He added that the state "shall endeavor to provide the facilities needed for the exercise of this freedom."[77]

However, given Iraq's intolerance of any kind of political dissent or criticism, it is hardly surprising that it reportedly prohibits unauthorized use of modems, which are a prerequisite for going online.[78]

The official press has been of two minds about the Internet, denouncing it as "one of the American means to enter every house in the world" while covering it favorably elsewhere.[79] Iraqi authorities have mounted web sites to disseminate official information. In April 1999 the Iraqi News Agency (INA) launched an Arabic and English site, <www.nisciraq.net/iraqnews>. The following month, *az-Zawra* became the first Iraqi newspaper to launch an online edition, hosting it on

---

[76] In response to Iraq's invasion of Kuwait in 1990, the Security Council prohibited all Iraqi exports and all imports except essential humanitarian items. U.N.S.C. resolution 687 (1991) conditioned the lifting of this embargo on a determination by the Security Council that the Iraqi government had complied with demands made in the resolution, including the destruction of its weapons of mass destruction and payment of reparations to Kuwait. Since 1995, the Security Council has allowed Iraq to export oil and use the proceeds to purchase humanitarian supplies, the selection and distribution of which is under U.N. supervision.

[77] Letter to Human Rights Watch from Nizar Hamdoon, the Permanent Representative of Iraq to the United Nations, June 1, 1998.

[78] Josh Friedman, a reporter for the Long Island, New York-based *Newsday*, told Human Rights Watch that when he and two other foreign journalists entered Iraq by land from Jordan in December 1998, Iraqi customs agents asked each one if he was carrying modems or satellite phones. They denied having modems. They were obliged to pay a fee of U.S. $300 for each satellite phone, which the agents then sealed with copper wire ostensibly to prevent their use except inside the press center of the Ministry of Communications in Baghdad. Telephone interview, January 11, 1999.

[79] For examples of Iraqi press commentary on the Internet, see the Mosaic Group, *The Global Diffusion of the Internet Project: An Initial Inductive Study*, March 1998, pp. 182-183, <www.agsd.com/gdi97/gdi97.html>.

a web site based in Jordan, <www.index.com.jo/iraqtoday/index.html>. Iraq's mission to the United Nations has long had a site of its own, <www.undp.org/missions/iraq/>.

Despite the damage inflicted on the country's infrastructure during the Gulf War and the ensuing sanctions, the government of Iraq could set up some sort of Internet link for its citizens if it had the will to do so, according to telecommunications experts. In Sulaymaniyeh, a northern city that is controlled by a Kurdish faction, beyond the reach of President Saddam Hussein's security forces, Internet access has been established using a small satellite dish. The local university connects to the Internet via that link.[80]

The sanctions regime has contributed to a drastic drop in Iraq's standard of living, health care, and education and set back its technological advancement. For many ordinary Iraqis, the hardships of daily survival have no doubt made Internet access seem a remote luxury. In addition, the U.N. sanctions regime has restricted the import of computers and peripherals, although the Security Council's sanctions committee has approved some purchases of computers for schools, and computer equipment is smuggled into the country and sold openly.[81]

The lack of Internet access is most regrettable at a time when Iraqis feel more cut off than ever from the outside world. The isolation and intellectual deprivation would no doubt be mitigated if Iraqis had given the opportunity to communicate inexpensively via e-mail and obtain from the World Wide Web and other online sources materials and information that is absent in their libraries and newsstands.

Iraq's opposition movements and parties in exile, as well as the Kurdish political parties that operate in the north of the country beyond Baghdad's control, maintain web sites. In addition, members of the Iraqi diaspora have created a cultural web site, <www.iraq.net>, that bills itself as "a small effort towards bringing Iraqis scattered around the globe, to one place, to share ideas, discuss Iraqi concerns, meet old friends, make new ones or simply...just to hang out!"[82]

---

[80] Telephone interview with Barham Saleh, Washington representative of the Patriotic Union of Kurdistan party, February 23, 1999.

[81] See Polly Sprenger, "Least Connected Nation Status, *Wired News Online*, December 17, 1998, <www.wired.com/news/news/politics/story/16904.html>, and Josh Friedman, "The Baghdad Marketplace: Despite Embargo, Smugglers Keep Rich Iraqis Supplied," *Newsday*, January 4, 1999, p. A14.

[82] Lisa Napoli, "Iraqi Exiles Reach for Home on Web Site," *New York Times*, February 20, 1997.

Jordan

Internet use has grown rapidly in Jordan, with the government extolling its virtues and imposing few restrictions. Authorities have been more tolerant toward news and comment online than toward traditional print and broadcast news media, with the result that Jordanians can obtain information from the Internet that is either taboo or ignored in the local print press.

Individuals, corporations, and organizations can establish Internet accounts easily. No form of government approval or registration is required to open an account or set up a web site. However, high phone and Internet access costs, including taxes and fees collected from ISPs, have kept the number of users—estimated at between 20,000 and 30,000—lower than it might otherwise be. In early 1999, a monthly account for a moderate user cost the equivalent of U.S. $70, including phone charges. Although there are six private ISPs, all must get their lines from the state telecommunications company and are captive to its relatively high pricing policies.

According to the government, "There is no blocking or censoring by the government of the content of any web sites or of electronic communications via newsgroups, e-mail or other Internet forums."[83] Human Rights Watch has heard no reports that contradict this assertion.

Privately run Internet cafés have proliferated in Amman and sprouted up in other cities.[84] The government states, "There are no special laws relating to their operation other than the standard licenses they have to obtain as any other business."[85] We are not aware of any form of government effort to restrict or monitor use of the Internet at cybercafés.

---

[83] Letter to Human Rights Watch from Marwan Muasher, Ambassador to the United States, May 21, 1998.

[84] A newspaper profile of cybercafés in Jordan reported that there were fourteen in Amman. Bassam Badareen, "Maqahi al-Internet fi Amman: al-Bahth 'an az-Zawja al-Munasaba...wa Afdhal at-Turuk li-Suna' al-Qunbala an-Nuwawiya," ("Cybercafés in Amman: Looking for a suitable wife...and the best way to build a nuclear weapon") *al-Quds al-Arabi*, September 29, 1998. An article in the October 6, 1998 *Al-Sharq al-Awsat* reported that there were fifteen cybercafés in Amman and nearly twenty elsewhere in Jordan. As reported in FBIS, October 29, 1998.

[85] Letter from Ambassador Muasher.

The Jordanian public has been able to obtain Internet access locally since 1996. The local providers offer national online newsgroups (electronic bulletin boards) and chat rooms.[86] In these forums, Jordanians have been able to converse about topics that the local press has covered gingerly if at all, such as the views and imprisonment of outspoken political dissident Leith Shbeilat (who himself has participated in online discussions), "honor" killings, Jordan's controversial peace treaty and relations with Israel, and armed attacks on Israeli targets.

Various government ministries have web sites and e-mail addresses, including the General Intelligence Department (<www.nic.gov.jo/gid>). At least one Internet service provider, NETS, invites subscribers to post comments and questions to participating government officials in an "Ask the Government" folder.

Jordanians have been able to go online to circumvent occasional prohibitions of foreign newspapers. On May 19, 1998, authorities banned the London-based daily *Al-Quds al-Arabi* indefinitely from importation. According to editor-in-chief Abdel-Barri Atwan, officials accused the paper of publishing stories hostile to Jordan, but did not specify which.[87] In their May 23 issues, various Jordanian dailies and weeklies ran advertisements from *Al-Quds al-Arabi* reminding readers that the full text of the newspaper was available daily at <www.alquds.co.uk>. According to editor Atwan, there were no reports of the site being blocked, and many Jordanians read the newspaper online. *Al-Quds* was later permitted to resume distribution of its print copies in Jordan.

Despite a relatively unfettered Internet, the increasing restrictions on freedom of expression and the press in Jordan[88] have cast a shadow over Internet use. It is widely believed that Jordanian security authorities read the comments posted in the chat rooms and bulletin boards established by Jordanian ISPs as forums on domestic issues. During 1996 the intelligence services summoned at least two persons for questioning over messages with political content that they posted on

---

[86] Jed Weiner, "Jordan and the Internet: Democracy Online?" *Middle East Insight*, May-June 1998, pp. 49-50.

[87] Telephone interview with Human Rights Watch, May 26, 1998.

[88] See Sa'eda Kilani, *Black Year for Democracy in Jordan: The 1998 Press and Publication Law* (Copenhagen: Euro-Mediterranean Human Rights Network, September 1998); Human Rights Watch, "Jordan: Clamping Down on Critics: Human Rights Violations," *A Human Rights Watch Report*, vol. 9, no. 12, October 1997; Human Rights Watch, "Jordan: A Death Knell for Free Expression?" *A Human Rights Watch Report*, vol. 9 , no. 5, June 1997.

bulletin boards or chat groups, according to Thamer A. Obeidat, an opposition political figure. Two Jordanian journalists separately confirmed his account to Human Rights Watch. Obeidat said the individuals did not want their identities disclosed for fear of reprisals.[89]

Human Rights Watch is unaware of such incidents recurring after 1996. However, several Jordanian Internet users told Human Rights Watch that while discussions about domestic political issues in the chat rooms and bulletins boards are more wide-ranging than the local print or broadcast media, users feared repercussions if they broke unspecified rules governing the way issues could be discussed. Marwan Joma, the general manager of NETS, one of the largest private ISPs, explained in a May 26, 1998 phone conversation with Human Rights Watch:

> There are very few rules, but NETS, being in Jordan, has to comply with local laws. This means users must not use foul language nor attack public figures. You can attack the policy of a certain minister, but you can't attack [them or other] subscribers personally. NETS doesn't screen [i.e., censor] messages, but we read the messages, like any other user, and if there's a [transgression] we send the user a reminder, and we can suspend them from a [forum].

Authorities directly pressured one online publication, *Amin* (Arab Media Internet Network, <www.amin.org>), which seeks to make available news and commentary not provided by the traditional media. *Amin*'s Jordan office was opened in 1997 as a project of the nonprofit international organization Internews (<www.internews.org>), which supports independent media in what it describes as "emerging democracies" and works to combat censorship. *Amin* quickly attracted some of the country's most talented journalists as contributors. In addition to providing links to the web sites of over one hundred Arab newspapers, magazines, radio, and television stations, *Amin* posts on its "Eye on Amman" link the latest communiqués from human rights organizations and coverage of Jordan's parliament, nongovernmental organizations, and women's issues.

According to Ra'ed al-Abed, then managing editor at *Amin*, the advent of the service provoked the ire of certain government officials. While some of Jordan's print publications have Internet editions, *Amin* was the first local media organ that is based online. During the first half of 1998, Bilal al-Tal, then-director of the government's Office of Press and Publications, phoned *Amin*'s offices on

---

[89] Letter to Human Rights Watch, May 17, 1998.

numerous occasions, warning the staff that they were not allowed to write about a particular topic, and that they were violating Jordanian law by operating without a license. However, al-Tal never formally initiated procedures to close down the agency. According to Fadi al-Qadi, the project director of *Amin* in Jordan, the agency applied for legal status as a nongovernmental organization in 1997, and in August 1998 that approval was granted.

A Jordanian journalist who is a fan of *Amin* commented to Human Rights Watch, "Because the laws are not clear, *Amin* presents a new challenge: it's like a newspaper but the [authorities] cannot treat it as a publication. Yet when they saw the content, they didn't like it and so they started calling them and telling them they were violating the press law."

According to a former editor at *Amin*, the agency's web site pushed the limits of what was appearing in Jordan's other news media, but did not feature any item that officials had explicitly ordered newspapers not to publish. He observed, "We have to be careful because operating in Jordan...we can't talk freely about the royal family, we wouldn't think about it as long as the laws are what they are. These are 'red lines.' If it comes to analysis, that's okay, but you cannot point fingers at any of the royal family."[90]

On September 1, 1998 the draconian Press and Publication Law took effect, restricting press freedom in a variety of ways. The broad language of this new legislation has been criticized by journalists and human rights activists in Jordan and overseas. Article 2, which defines "publication" as "any media in which meanings, words, or ideas are expressed in any way," could easily be interpreted to apply to online publications, although authorities have not to our knowledge explicitly stated this to be the case. Features of the new law that restrict free expression include requirements that:

- private non-daily publications secure a minimum capital of 100,000 Jordanian dinars (about U.S.$140,000); dailies must have a minimum capital of 500,000 dinars within a three-month period in order to publish, a sevenfold increase from the previous law (article 13);

- publications "refrain from publishing anything that conflicts with the principles of freedom, national responsibility, human rights and values of the Arab and Islamic nation" (article 5); and

---

[90] Telephone interview with Human Rights Watch, May 14, 1998.

- periodicals [which are also defined in a way that could include online publications] refrain from publishing any materials containing content deemed objectionable, including anything that "disparages the King and the Royal family...infringes on the judiciary or undermines its independence...[and that] encourages perversion or leads to moral corruption" (article 37).

Violations of article 37 make a periodical subject to fines of not less than 5,000 dinars (article 47) and possible court-ordered closure (article 50). As of May 1999, the Press and Publications Law had been invoked only once to suspend a print publication;[91] its effect on online media remained unclear.

Morocco

The government of Morocco does not restrict access to the Internet or censor content, according to several Internet users interviewed in Morocco. Accounts are easily obtained from dozens of private service providers, and users can access the unfiltered World Wide Web from home, the office, or one of many cybercafés operating in the big cities.

Yet Internet use has grown slowly since it was introduced in late 1995. Contrary to official claims of more than 40,000 regular Internet users in a country of 28 million,[92] the private Internet Association estimated the number of subscribers at 8,000 and the number of regular users at 12,000.[93] According to the association's president, Chakib Lahrichi, the slow growth is due not to government restrictions but rather to high costs for users, the absence of a national policy to promote Internet development, and unfair advantages enjoyed by the state-

---

[91] A court of first instance suspended *Al-Majd* weekly on February 14, 1999. Publication resumed after an appeals court overturned the suspension, but the charges against the weekly were not dropped.

[92] The web site of the state-controlled Itissalat al-Maghrib telecommunications utility, <http://onpt.net.ma/>, accessed May 12, 1999, claimed "more than 40,000 regular users in Morocco."

[93] E-mail communication from association president Chakib Lahrichi to Human Rights Watch, May 12, 1999.

controlled telecommunications company Itissalat al-Maghrib (IAM) in its competition with private ISPs.[94]

In early 1998, Internet access in Morocco cost about U.S. $40-50 per month for a subscription that included fifteen hours online plus the cost of the telephone connection (approximately $2 per hour). This cost was quite high for a country with one of the region's lowest per capita gross national products.[95] By 1999 the average subscriptions had dropped to about $20 per month for unlimited access, with telephone charges remaining at about $2 per hour.

Lahrichi, who heads a major Casablanca-based private ISP called L&L Technologies, pointed out that Internet growth was impeded by the structure of telecommunications in the country. Private ISPs, he said, must use the lines and international gateway maintained by IAM. For the services it provides them, IAM "imposed whatever prices it wants" while competing with them as an ISP itself.

Lahrichi said, however, that he was aware of no government-imposed blocking or filtering of web pages, newsgroups, or e-mail. ISPs provided Internet access for anyone who could pay for it and were not required by the government to furnish any information about their customers. With respect to Morocco's cybercafés, Lahrichi said anyone could open one and he had not heard of any being the object of government pressure or surveillance.

Karl Stanzick, who manages an ISP called MTDS (Morocco Trade and Development Services) in Rabat, said "there is no 'usage contract' which needs to be signed or agreed to by the Internet subscriber whether purchasing an hour in the cybercafé, a dial-up account, or a leased line." Stanzick added that no government approval is required to obtain an Internet account or post a web site, and "all Internet subscribers in Morocco can be completely anonymous if they wish." He said the authorities have not imposed on ISPs any form of legal liability for materials they carry, and he was unaware of any ISP that had been punished for "objectionable" content. Stanzick remarked, however, that the "red lines" that inhibit political commentary in traditional media—the taboos on questioning the institution of the monarchy and Morocco's claim to the Western Sahara, and on

---

[94] Interview with Human Rights Watch, Casablanca, April 30, 1998 and e-mail to Human Rights Watch, May 12, 1999. See also Ghassan Khaber, "Internet au Maroc: Deux ans et toujours à tâtonner," *L'Économiste* (Morocco), January 15, 1998.

[95] Morocco's GNP per capita was U.S.$1,250 in 1997, according to The World Bank, *World Development Report, 1998/99*, p.191.

"insulting" the King or Islam—also limit what Moroccans are willing to post in public chat-rooms and electronic bulletin boards.[96]

The owner of an Internet café in a major Moroccan city, who requested anonymity, said that there had been no interference by authorities concerning what Internet users could do while at the establishment. He said clients could access anything they wished. A sample web search at the café for pro-Polisario[97] perspectives on the Western Sahara conflict turned up many sites, such as <www.arso.org>, containing material that would never appear in the Moroccan print or broadcast media.

The only instance of censorship that the café had experienced occurred in February 1997, when the owner said he received a written order from the regional police headquarters warning him that a particular compact disc software program entitled "3D Atlas" was banned in Morocco. Although the order did not explain the reason for the prohibition, the owner said he had been given to understand that it was due to the way that this software presented the issue of sovereignty over the Western Sahara.

Although the government of Morocco did not reply to Human Rights Watch's written questions about Internet policies, it forwarded in June 1998 a fact-sheet about Internet use in the Kingdom. It stated that sixteen government ministries and agencies maintain web sites and seven Moroccan newspapers are online.[98]

Saudi Arabia

In January 1999, Saudi Arabia began allowing its public to access the Internet through local service providers. It did so while promising to implement what would be the region's most ambitious plan to block the flow of "undesirable" data online.

Saudi Arabia has had an Internet connection since 1994, but restricted its use to state academic, medical, and research institutions. Saudi citizens and residents

---

[96] E-mail communications to Human Rights Watch, May 21, 1998 and January 12, 1999.

[97] The Popular Front for the Liberation of Saguia el-Hamra and Rio de Oro, known as the Polisario Front, is the Western Saharan liberation movement. Morocco has asserted sovereignty over the territory and has been fighting a war against the Polisario since the mid-1970s.

[98] The French embassy in Rabat maintains a handy directory of online addresses in Morocco, at <www.ambafrance-ma.org/public/webmaroc.htm.>.

were free, however, to purchase computers and modems, could connect to the Internet through dial-up service to foreign ISPs, and launch web sites on foreign servers. But international calls to ISPs were expensive: to Bahrain the charge was U.S. $0.60–0.80 per minute, and to the U.S. and Europe $1.70–$2.10 per minute. Still, according to one estimate, some 30,000 Saudis were accessing the Internet in this fashion.[99] The Saudi public could also subscribe to local networks such as al-Naseej (<www.naseej.com.sa>), which provided domestic and international e-mail, links to domestic databases and "chat rooms" for its own subscribers—but no access to the World Wide Web.

Although state institutions were first connected to the Internet in 1994 and King Fahd had approved public Internet access in 1997, it was not until January 1999 that local ISPs began connecting ordinary citizens. This delay was due in large part to the self-proclaimed determination of authorities to establish a system for controlling the flow of information online.

Officials of the Saudi government and the King Abdul-Aziz City for Science and Technology (KACST)—the Riyadh-based state institution charged with coordinating Internet policy—declined to respond to repeated written, phone, and e-mail invitations from Human Rights Watch to provide information. However, they made their intention to exercise control over Internet content clear in numerous press interviews. Saleh Abdulrahman Al-'Adhel, president of the KACST, said in February 1998:

> A standing committee has been formed and approved by the government to protect society from material on the Internet that violates Islam or encroaches on our traditions and culture. This committee will determine which sites are immoral, such as pornographic sites and others, and will bar subscribers from entering such sites. There are many bad things on Internet. That is why we have created a mechanism to prevent such things from reaching our society so that a home subscriber to this service can be reassured. We have programs, software, and hardware that prevent the entry of material that corrupts or that harms our Muslim values, tradition, and culture. We also created a "fire wall" or barrier to prevent other quarters from breaching our sites. That is why we have not rushed into

---

[99] "Saudi Arabia ready to cruise the information superhighway," Agence France-Presse, July 15, 1998.

providing this service. We first want to make sure we eliminate all negative aspects of the Internet.[100]

That objective was endorsed early on by Saudi Arabia's Council of Ministers when it called for a fire wall, maintained by the KACST, to keep the public from accessing "inappropriate" information.[101] The council also prepared a set of broad and vaguely defined restrictions on Internet content and usage. Its Decision number 163, made public in May 1998, requires ISPs and users to refrain from "using the network for illegitimate purposes such as, for example, pornography and gambling;...carrying out any activities violating the social, cultural, political, media, economic, and religious values of the Kingdom of Saudi Arabia; sending or receiving coded information unless after obtaining the necessary licenses from the administration of the network in question; [and] introducing others into the usage accounts or briefing them on the secret number of the user."[102]

Authorities have divulged few details of the technical means and criteria used to block content. According to one press report, "Industry insiders claim King Abdul-Aziz City for Science and Technology will simply provide a list of desirable sites, officially sanctioned by an internal committee. All other sites will be banned by default. In other words, the user will not be able to type in the URL of any site that he/she wants to visit, but rather only be able to pick from an officially sanctioned list."[103] If accurate, this would be the world's most restrictive regime of web-site filtering. The London-based daily *Al-Sharq al-Awsat* reported that the

---

[100] Quoted in *'Ukaz* newspaper, February 24, 1998, as reported in FBIS, February 27, 1998.

[101] The Mosaic Group, *The Global Diffusion of the Internet Project: An Initial Inductive Study*, March 1998, p. 216, or <www.agsd.com/gdi97/gdi97.html>. An updated version, dated February 1999, of the *Inductive Study*'s chapter on Saudi Arabia can be found at <www.agsd.com/gdiff/gdiff4>. The term "fire wall" connotes various tools that restrict users' access to online data, either in proprietary sites or on the Internet. It can be set up as a security device to prevent unauthorized access to computer systems or as a censorship device to block user access to online materials that a government or fire-wall operator seeks to place off-limits.

[102] Quoted in *Al-Jazira* newspaper, May 6, 1998, as reported in FBIS, May 12, 1998.

[103] *IT News*, November 4, 1998, <www.ditnet.co.ae/html/newsnov/ newsnov0198.html>.

Saudis planned to contract with U.S. firms to bolster their censorship efforts by furnishing on a continuous basis the addresses of web sites deemed offensive.[104]

Saudi Arabia allows private ISPs. In November 1998 the government approved applications from some forty companies seeking to provide Internet services. However, all ISPs operating in the Kingdom are to be linked to a main server at the KACST, which has the country's sole gateway to the World Wide Web.[105] This structure would certainly facilitate any possible efforts by the government to monitor and limit Internet use and content.

Two months after local ISPs began offering access, Al-'Adhel affirmed that the KACST was "blocking undesirable web sites" by using what he called "very fast computer programs." He denied that the KACST had prohibited any applications, such as chat services—"unless [they were] linked to pornographic sites."[106]

Although official explanations of content filtering have focused on materials deemed offensive to conservative Muslim sensibilities, Saudi blocking apparently extends to political sites. In early 1999, the site of at least one exiled dissident group, the Committee against Corruption in Saudi Arabia (<www.saudhouse.com>), was reportedly blocked.

Users who attempt to access banned sites reportedly receive warnings on their computer screens that their access attempts are being logged.[107] Saudi authorities have also tried to thwart user efforts to circumvent censorship. The URL of a popular web-based anti-censorship proxy server, Osiris, is blocked in the Kingdom, along with at least three "mirror" sites, according to Brian Ristuccia, who manages

---

[104] "Internet Service in the Arab World," *Al-Sharq al-Awsat*, October 4, 1998, as reported in FBIS, October 29, 1998.

[105] The regulations on ISPs forbid them from establishing any linkage to the Internet except via the KACST. The rules were published in the May 6, 1998 *al-Jazira* daily, as reported in FBIS, May 12, 1998.

[106] Nasser Salih al-Sarami, "Problems and Possibilities; Internet in the Kingdom," *Saudi Gazette*, March 13, 1999.

[107] Jehl, "The Internet's 'Open Sesame,'" *New York Times*.

the site.[108] And a web site offering anonymizing services, <www.anonymizer. com>, is also blocked, according to the company's president, Lance Cottrell.[109]

The pricing structure for Internet accounts that was announced by the KACST for ISP charges appears moderate to high, depending on whether the ISPs choose to offer rates closer to the low or high end of the permissible range set by the KACST. Saudi newspapers on November 10, 1999 quoted KACST officials saying they had agreed to a minimum ISP charge of 1.5 riyals an hour (1 riyal equals U.S.$0.27) and a maximum of 4.5 riyals, along with a fixed monthly charge of between 100 and 150 riyals. An additional dial-up charge of 4.5 riyals per hour would be paid to Saudi Telecom.[110] (Saudi Telecom is a state monopoly, although the first steps toward privatizing it were taken in 1998.) Thus, a light user, one who spends five hours online per month, would pay a monthly rate of between U.S. $36–$44.

Syria
Despite an online connection established in 1997 and frequent pro-Internet statements, Syria remains the only connected country in the region that has yet to allow its public local access to the Internet. But a few thousand modems are said to be in Syrian hands, allowing those who have access to them to maintain Internet accounts with ISPs in Lebanon and elsewhere.[111] Syrians who are able to travel to neighboring Jordan or Lebanon can patronize cybercafés; none exist in Syria.

The government of President Hafez al-Asad did not respond to Human Rights Watch's letter requesting information on Internet policies. Its go-slow approach is consistent however with its efforts to suppress all forms of expression deemed critical of how the country is governed. All newspapers and broadcast media are

---

[108] E-mail communication from Brian Ristuccia to Human Rights Watch, January 7, 1999 and March 11, 1999.

[109] Cottrell, "Commercial Anonymity."

[110] "Saudi Sets Limits to Internet Provider Charges," Reuters, November 10, 1998.

[111] Joseph Contreras, "The Information Age Dawns, Championed by Assad's Son," *Newsweek*, April 26, 1999.

tightly controlled, and hundreds of political prisoners remain behind bars, many of them serving long terms for peaceful dissent.[112]

Official discourse about the Internet has been ambivalent, favorable to its potential as a tool of communication while mindful of its purported social dangers. A February 1998 article in the official *Tishrin* daily advocated an Arab strategy to develop Internet use in order to counteract the heavy Internet presence of Israeli sources and viewpoints. The author called for "prepar[ing] national and Arab plans to introduce the Internet culture to all people" and provid[ing] Internet connections at symbolic rates."[113] Since 1997, some official and semi-official Syrian institutions have been linked to the Internet. Some have established a presence on the Web, including the Syrian Arab News Agency (<www.sana.org>), *Tishrin* daily (<www.teshreen.com>), and the Syrian Computer Society (<www.scs-syria.org>).

Syria's most prominent advocate of the Internet is Bashar al-Asad, the president's son. He chairs the Syrian Computer Society. According to one news report, Bashar's position in favor of public access to the Internet has been opposed by security and intelligence officials.[114]

A spokesman for the Syrian Computer Society, Saadallah Agha al-Kalaa, justified the slow approach to extending access beyond state institutions. "Our problem is...we are a traditional society, and we have to know if there is something that cannot fit with our society. We have to make it safe." He added, "We want to have Internet with a minimum of problems, so the solution was to go by stages. Where the need is most important, in universities, centers of research, ministries of economy...all these sites are connected now." Kalaa insisted that the government's reluctance to open up Syria to the Internet reflected social concern

---

[112] See the Syria chapter in Human Rights Watch, *Human Rights Watch World Report 1999* (New York: Human Rights Watch, 1998), pp. 372-376, and Reporters sans Frontières, "Journalists Tortured in Syria," March 1999.

[113] Husayn al-Ibrahim, "The Internet and Informatics in the Arab-Israeli Conflict," *Tishrin*, February 23, 1998, as reported in FBIS, March 1, 1998.

[114] Douglas Jehl, "In Syria, Only the Population is Growing," *New York Times*, January 25, 1998.

about Internet content rather than political fears about the free exchange of information.[115]

In an article sympathetically explaining Syria's "cautious" approach to the Internet, Amr Salem, a co-founder of the SCS, wrote:

In order for President Assad to feel comfortable promoting a particular technology, it must meet the following criteria:

1. It should benefit the majority of the Syrian people. Technology geared toward the elite is not favored because such people have the resources and means to get what they want without government assistance.
2. It should not disrupt the social structure or adversely affect the middle class, and must be within the means of the masses.
3. It should have a direct impact on Syria's overall social and economic development.
4. It should not jeopardize Syrian independence or security concerns.[116]

According to one news report, the few Syrians who have access to the Internet because they work at connected state institutions do not have unfettered access: Syria's sole service provider, the monopoly Syrian Telecommunications Establishment (STE), blocks access to web sites containing information or pictures deemed offensive.[117] Human Rights Watch has no information concerning the type of content that is blocked. As noted above, the Syrian government and the Syrian Computer Society did not respond to written queries from Human Rights Watch concerning restrictions on Web access and content.

In early 1999 there were once again press reports that public access was imminent. Reuters reported that a public domestic e-mail service would be made available on a limited basis in February, but would be via a special server at the state telecommunications center that "would allow control of incoming and

---

[115] Jack Redden, "Internet Arrives in Syria, But Not without Limits," Reuters, July 10, 1998. An e-mail sent by Human Rights Watch to the SCS seeking comment on the Reuters story went unanswered.

[116] Amr Salem, "Syria's Cautious Embrace," *Middle East Insight*, March-April 1999, pp. 49-50.

[117] "Internet Service in the Arab World," *Al-Sharq al-Awsat*, October 6, 1998, as reported in FBIS, October 29, 1998.

outgoing services, including the ability to block contact with destinations regarded as undesirable."[118] As of May 1999, public access was still unavailable.

Tunisia

The relative length of this section should not be taken to mean that Tunisia's restrictions on the Internet are more onerous than elsewhere. It is a reflection, rather, of the fact that Tunisia has the region's most detailed Internet legislation, it has explicitly extended its press law to cover the Internet, and the government has provided Human Rights Watch with much information on which to comment.

Tunisian policy reflects deep ambivalence toward the Internet. President Zine al-Abidine Ben Ali has extolled the importance of developing information technologies, including the Internet, and of making it widely accessible.[119] Official agencies have an active presence on the World Wide Web (see <www.ministeres.tn>), and Tunisian television and radio are broadcast live online (<www.tunisiatv.com> and <www.radiotunis.com>). The government has been improving the Internet infrastructure by widening the bandwidth, among other measures. The rates charged for Internet access and phone use have been dropping, along with customs duties on imported computer equipment, making Internet access more affordable.

Tunisian authorities say the country's Internet-specific legislation is designed to "promote" the delivery of Internet services and "prepare Tunisia for the age of the Information Society." The legislation aims to "furnish access to Internet services to all who want it, at the same quality and the same price" and to "stimulate the private sector, within a framework of loyal competition, to commercialize Internet access services and develop web-site hosting capacity." The government also "aims to connect all university and scientific research institutions to the Internet, to be followed in stages by the connection of high schools ("*lycées et collèges"*) between now and the end of the current [five-year] plan [2001], with the intention of connecting primary schools to this network in the subsequent stage."

---

[118] "Syria Plans Controlled E-mail Service," Reuters, January 6, 1999.

[119] Unless otherwise noted, all citations are from the reply by the Tunisian government to Human Rights Watch's questions, reprinted in Appendix C. It was translated from French by Human Rights Watch.

While Tunisia's Internet regulations establish standards and rules for an emerging commercial sector, they also reflect the government's restrictive approach to freedom of expression and intolerance of dissent. In Tunisia, all news media promote the official line and avoid news and commentary that imply criticism of government policies. Smaller publications have only slightly more leeway. Political and human rights activists who have criticized repressive measures have been jailed, penalized at their workplaces, prevented from traveling abroad, or otherwise harassed. Pervasive police surveillance of activists, ex-prisoners, and their families reinforces a climate of fear and self-censorship.[120]

Tunisia's press code contains many articles that restrict the content of what may be said or published. Article 62 forbids the distribution, sale, display, or possession of "leaflets, publications, or books, of domestic or of foreign origin, that are of a nature that could disturb public order and good morals." The provisions most frequently used to punish critical speech are article 49, which criminalizes the dissemination of "false" information, and articles 50-53, which deal with defamation. Article 49 states:

The publication, dissemination or reproduction by any means of false news, information which has been fabricated, falsified or wrongly attributed to others, if made in bad faith and if it has either disturbed or is likely to disturb public order, may be punished by imprisonment of two months to three years and/or a fine of 100-2,000 dinars [equivalent to U.S. $93-1,860].

Article 50 states that defamation has occurred if there is "a public allegation or attribution of a fact that harms the honor or esteem (*considération*) of a person or state agency to whom the fact was attributed." Defamation is punishable by up to three years in prison and a fine of up to 1,200 dinars if the offending material is published "directly or by means of reproduction" (article 50). The code specifies various public entities that can be thus defamed, including "the public order, the courts, the ground, sea and air forces, public agencies and public administrations." Defamation is punishable by the same penalties if it is committed against one or more "members of the government, one or more deputies, civil servants," and other

---

[120] For general information about the state of free expression, see Article 19, *Surveillance and Repression: Freedom of Expression in Tunisia* (London: Article 19, May 1998), Human Rights Watch, *Human Rights Watch World Report 1999* (New York: Human Rights Watch, December 1998); and the U.S. Department of State's *Country Reports on Human Rights Practices* for 1998.

public servants "by virtue of their functions or their status." The truth of the allegation can be used as a defense, but not in all situations.

The use of these articles to prosecute journalists and others illustrates what the organization Article 19 characterized as "the state using the law to prevent public discussion of matters of great public import but which are in some way critical of the government's performance."[121] One example is the three-year prison sentence imposed on human rights activist Khemaïs Ksila for a communiqué he distributed in September 1997 denouncing government repression.

A state agency, the Agence Tunisienne d'Internet (ATI), coordinates Internet policies and services and acts as a kind of super-ISP. It leases Internet access to several private ISPs, including two that are licensed to offer Internet services to the private sector and individuals, Global Net (<www.gnet.tn>) and PlaNet. These two companies are reportedly controlled by persons close to the President. All private ISPs merely retail Internet access to customers; all communications, domestic and international, reportedly go through the ATI and the state telecommunications network. The ATI maintains control over all of the protocols and the country's only international gateway.

The main piece of legislation governing the Internet is a decree issued on March 22, 1997, hereinafter "the Internet decree."[122] It followed by eight days a decree that covers telecommunications services more generally.[123]

The telecommunications decree provides the following:

- The press code shall apply to the production, provision, distribution and storing of information through telecommunication means [including the Internet] (article 1).
- All ISPs must obtain a license from the Ministry of Communications (article 7).

---

[121] Article 19, *Surveillance and Repression: Freedom of Expression in Tunisia* (London: Article 19, May 1998), p. 71.

[122] Arrêté du ministre des communications du 22 mars 1997, portant approbation du cahier des charges fixant les clauses particulières à la mise en œuvre et l'exploitation des services à valeur ajoutée des télécommunications de type INTERNET.

[123] Décret no. 97-501 du 14 mars 1997 relatif aux services à valeur ajoutée des télécommunications.

- A "Commission on Telecommunications Services" shall review each application to operate an ISP company; the commission includes representatives from the ministries of defense and interior, as well as officials holding posts related to communications, information and computer sciences (article 8).

The Internet decree imposes the following rules:

- Each ISP must designate a director who "assumes responsibility...for the content of pages and Web pages and sites that the ISP is requested to host on its servers (article 9, paragraph 3). Internet users and those who maintain web sites and servers are also responsible for infractions of the law (article 9, paragraph 4);
- Each ISP must submit, on a monthly basis, a list of its Internet subscribers to the "public operator" (the state-run ATI) (article 8, paragraph 5); if the ISP closes down or stops providing services, it must "without delay" turn over to the "public operator" a complete set of its archives ("*l'ensemble des supports d'archivage*") as well as the means to read it (article 9, paragraph 7).
- The "director" is to maintain "constant oversight" of the content on the ISP's servers, to insure that no information remains on the system that is contrary to "public order and good morals" (*"l'ordre publique"* and *"bonnes mœurs,"* the same phrases that are found in article 62 of the press code, which provides for the confiscation of publications).

The Internet decree also bars encryption without prior approval from the authorities (article 11). A September 1997 decree on encryption requires that persons or service providers who wish to encrypt data must submit an application to the Ministry of Communications and provide the keys needed to decrypt the data.[124] The ministry decides on the application after consulting the Commission on Telecommunications, cited above.

The contract that institutional subscribers sign when obtaining services from the ATI imposes further government controls. Most remarkably, it requires users to sign that they will "use the Internet only for scientific, technological or

---

[124] Arrêté du ministre des communications du 9 septembre 1997 fixant les conditions d'utilisation du cryptage dans l'exploitation des services à valeur ajoutée des télécommunications.

commercial purposes that are strictly related to the activity of the client, in strict conformity with the rules in effect." The contract also requires that clients:

- "Disclose to the ATI all accounts that have been opened for users and those having access";
- "Prevent remote access to its network by external users who lack prior authorization from the ATI"; and
- "Inform the ATI of any change in address, equipment, and user."

The ATI reserves the right to suspend Internet service without notice if the subscriber engages in any use that is "improper or contrary to the conditions laid out" in the contract. The agency also has the right under the contract to conduct site visits to ensure that the equipment connected to the Internet is being used "in conformity with the rules and laws as well as to ensure they are being used properly." (Embassies and international institutions are exempted from this provision.)

Commentary on Tunisia's Legislation

Responsibility of ISP for content: The imposition of legal responsibility on the ISP, and specifically on its designated "responsible person," for the web sites it hosts, poses a threat to online freedom of expression. It does so by imposing a regulatory burden on providers even though they cannot realistically police the web sites they host, many of which are revised daily by their authors. If enforced, this provision is likely to slow or reduce the flow of data online.

The government, in its letter to Human Rights Watch, states that ISPs are responsible only for the content of web sites but not for the content of e-mail messages or newsgroup postings. But responsibility for newsgroup content seems encompassed by the section of the Internet decree stipulating that the ISP must allow nothing to "remain" on its servers that harms "public order and good morals." This broad and vague wording seems intended to compel ISPs to err on the side of censoring content so as not to run afoul of the regulations.

Furnishing lists of subscribers to the government. The government explains that ISPs must submit monthly the names of its subscribers in order to facilitate maintaining a statistical base and directory of Internet users. The government states that ISPs must otherwise keep information about users and their usage confidential.

The obligation to furnish the government with subscriber lists infringes on the privacy and anonymity rights of Internet users. In the compilation of a user directory or a database we can find no interest compelling enough to warrant infringement of the rights of users who do not wish to provide this information. The mandatory delivery to the authorities of such information, which could facilitate electronic surveillance, can only inhibit Tunisians wishing to express themselves or receive information online.

ATI's Contract Restricts Users' Rights. The contract presented to institutional clients by the ATI restricts their right to seek and access information online. The requirement that they use it only for "scientific, technological or commercial purposes that are strictly related to the activity of the client" apparently bars them from using the Internet account for personal or other business, under penalty of cancellation of the contract. The contract also violates the privacy of users by requiring that they inform the ATI of all persons who have access to their accounts.

***

In early 1998, the number of Tunisians online was estimated between 3,000 and 5,000. This figure seemed low for a middle-income country of seven million with a relatively high rate of educational attainment and a good phone system. There were, moreover, few Internet accounts at universities, which are all public institutions, and at nongovernmental organizations. These two sectors exhibit relatively high rates of Internet connectivity in many other middle-income countries.

Beginning in 1998, the government has taken measures to accelerate the growth of Internet use. Prices for Internet accounts dropped through 1998 and the first half of 1999. Consulted on May 17, 1999, the web site of PlaNet advertised a rate for households of about U.S. $17 per month for unlimited usage during off-peak hours, a huge drop from two years earlier. In early 1999, articles in the local press forecast that, thanks to government initiatives, the number of users would reach 30,000 during 1999.

Human Rights Watch interviewed several Tunisians who concurred that the process of obtaining Internet access had grown more efficient and reliable since 1998. They said that prior to 1998, few Tunisians had access to the Internet and that applications were often delayed or simply never processed. These individuals, who are not outspoken dissidents and requested anonymity, all said they believed that police scrutiny of each application and government wariness toward allowing widespread Internet access explained these past delays in processing applications, the absence of Internet cafés until late 1998 (see below) and, more generally, the low number of users in the country.

According to the government, "access for individuals, organizations and companies to Internet services is made available simply by applying to the ISP of their choice." The applicant is not required to notify or obtain permission from any governmental entity. However, almost all of those we interviewed said they knew of persons who had applied for Internet services in past years and who had waited months for a response, or who received no response at all. They also said they had heard of persons whose accounts were terminated without explanation. A university professor told Human Rights Watch in October 1998 how his application was ignored: "Two years ago, I received mail, inviting me to apply for an Internet account. It contained a copy of a contract, which said I would be responsible for how the account was used, and said I would have to pledge to use it only for professional purposes, and so on. I filled it out and sent it in, but never received any response."

A professor at the law school in Sousse told Human Rights Watch in August 1998 that few professors in Tunisia have Internet accounts; he said that his law faculty had no Internet account. A professor who teaches at the University of Tunis told Human Rights Watch that some academic departments were given a single Internet account, with a warning to the senior faculty member that he or she was responsible for all use of the account. A similar warning was delivered to the executive director of one of the few nongovernmental organizations to enjoy Internet access.

Without exception, the Tunisians we interviewed said they believed the government monitored e-mail correspondence. None of them could cite concrete evidence for this, but said they made this assumption because of the level of police surveillance of telephone conversations and other aspects of Tunisian life,[125] and incidents where e-mails were lost or delayed by one day or longer while en route.

Tunisia's blocking of web sites is another manifestation of its vigilance over the flow of information online. The government, in its letter to Human Rights Watch, avoids any allusion to blocking web sites on the basis of political content and suggests that any blocking is motivated by moral and privacy concerns:

---

[125] The U.S. State Department's *Country Reports on Human Rights Practices* for 1998 reported, "There were numerous reports of government interception of facsimile and computer-transmitted communications."

Tunisia is committed to the principle of preserving moral values and the protection of personal privacy. Web sites, electronic communications, and other online forums that do not comply with these principles (pedophilia, pornography, etc.) are in violation of the law. Tunisia is following with interest the debates over this question on an international scale, in order to find appropriate solutions.

In fact, authorities also block some web sites containing information critical of Tunisia's human rights record. Internet users in Tunisia reported that they could not access the web sites of Amnesty International (<www.amnesty.org>) and the Committee To Protect Journalists (<www.cpj.org>), a New York-based group that in 1998 and 1999 cited President Ben Ali on a list of press freedom's ten greatest "enemies." One user said he believed that authorities had also blocked <www.mygale.org>, a web site that offered free web-page hosting and sometimes carried material on Tunisia (there were, for example, links to many human rights reports critical of Tunisia at <www.mygale.org/~maghreb>). Another user reported in late 1998 that the site <www.i-france.com/EFAI>, which contains the texts of Amnesty International reports in French, was also blocked. The web site of Reporters sans Frontières (<www.rsf.fr>) was also blocked, according to the small independent Tunisian magazine *al-Mawqif*.[126]

Absent a government confirmation, it is not always possible to confirm that a site is inaccessible due to blocking rather than to technical problems. However, in the case of the Amnesty International web site, at least, the evidence clearly points to intentional blocking.

A private firm with friendly ties to the Tunisian government mounted a web site with a URL that appeared likely to fool persons trying to access Amnesty International information. The site, <www.amnesty-tunisia.org>, closely tracked the government's own rhetoric on human rights while avoiding any mention of Amnesty International. Tunisian authorities denied any role in the web site.[127] The domain name is registered to the Paris-based Euromed Group (<www.euromed.com>). Euromed chairman Raghid el-Chammah, who conducts business in Tunisia, insisted in a press interview that the web site was his own

---

[126] Tayeb Ma'li, "Fukku al-Riqaba 'an al-Internet!" ("End Censorship of the Internet!") *al-Mawqif*, January 1999.

[127] "Web: l'affirmation d'Amnesty est 'ridicule', selon l'ambassade de Tunisie," Agence France-Presse, November 27, 1998.

project and that he chose the word "amnesty" because it was appropriate for a human rights site and not because it was the name of a prominent organization critical of Tunisia's record on rights.[128] In a counter-offensive, Amnesty International launched a web site, <www.amnesty.org/tunisia>, that juxtaposed the pro-Tunisian positions found at <www.amnesty-tunisia.org> with its own assessment of the human rights situation.[129] The contents of <www.amnesty-tunisia.org> was subsequently withdrawn and replaced by a statement condemning Amnesty International's tactics as an effort "to show its new prowess in cyberpropaganda." The original contents were moved to a new site, <www.rights-tunisia.org>.

In late 1998, the first Internet cafés opened in Tunisia, long after they had proliferated in Morocco, Egypt, Jordan, and elsewhere. According to a European journalist who visited two of them in greater Tunis in February 1999, the "PubliNet" cafés had certain local characteristics. First, in both locations, the monitors were all positioned so that their screens were visible to the administrator of the café, thus diminishing user privacy. Second, in one of the cafés, clients were asked to present identity documents, and in the other location they were asked their names and addresses. This requirement deprives users of their right to use the Internet anonymously and is apparently intended to ensure some oversight of Internet use at these new public points of access.

United Arab Emirates

The United Arab Emirates, one of the world's wealthiest and most technologically modern countries,[130] can also claim to being the most wired state in the Arab world. As of October 1988 it had 52,000 subscribers and 143,000 users,

---

[128] Pamela Mendels, "Rights Group Fights a Foe with Frames," *New York Times Cybertimes* (online), February 16, 1999, <www.nytimes.com/library/tech/99/02/cyber/articles/16amnesty.html>. See also Roula Khalaf, "Amnesty Defends Itself," *Financial Times*, February 13, 1999.

[129] Amnesty International press release, February 1, 1999, ACT 83/01/99.

[130] World Bank, *World Development Report, 1998/99* (Oxford: Oxford University Press, published for the World Bank, 1999), and International Telecommunication Union, *World Telecommunication Development Report*, 3rd ed., 1996/97 (Geneva: International Telecommunication Union, 1997). The ITU web site, <www.itu.inti>, has links to a variety of country-by-country telecommunications statistics.

according to one estimate.[131] The country has numerous cy'
to the *Middle East Internet Directory* for 1998, the largest numbe____
sites.[132] Government ministries maintain sophisticated web sites and a pu____
think-tank, the Emirates Center for Strategic Studies and Resear____
(<www.ecssr.ac.ae>), hosts international conferences on the information revolution
in the region.[133]

The U.A.E. has at the same time been the regional leader in advocating
censorship of the Web through the use of high-tech means. An official with
Etisalat (the Emirates Telecommunications Corporation), which is the country's
state-controlled telecommunications monopoly and sole Internet provider, was
quoted in 1997 as saying, "Singapore has succeeded to a great extent in its drive to
control harm done by the Internet. Why cannot we?"[134]

Dial-up users in the U.A.E. do not access the Internet directly. They dial in to
a proxy server maintained by Etisalat. The proxy will refuse access to web sites if
the URL requested is on a list of banned sites, or if a content check of the site by
the proxy server turns up objectionable material.

Government officials, who acknowledged that this censorship regime was
administered by the state telecommunications company, insisted that its sole
purpose was to block pornographic sites. A senior official in the Ministry of
Information and Culture, who was interviewed on condition his name not be used,
told Human Rights Watch in a telephone interview on June 10, 1998:

> There is no restriction on the political, social, economic side. Politically,
> in the U.A.E., we do not hold value for censorship, especially political or

---

[131] Survey published in the November 1998 *Internet al-Alam al-Arabi* magazine
(<www.iawmag.com>, summarized in English at <www.ditnet.co.ae/me_internet.html>.

[132] Although one estimate ranked the U.A.E. highest in absolute numbers of users,
Qatar, with its smaller population, had a higher proportion of its population using the
Internet: 3.1 percent as opposed to 2.99 percent in January 1998. See Appendix A.

[133] It sponsored, for example, "The Impact of the Information and Communications
Revolution on Society and State in the Arab World," January 4-7, 1997. The conference
papers were published as *The Information Revolution and the Arab World: Its Impact on
State and Society* (Abu Dhabi: The Emirates Center for Strategic Studies and Research,
1998).

[134] Reuters, January 25, 1997.

censorship of ideas: we don't believe in that. You can access on the Internet any material, from Israel or anywhere. The whole idea [of the proxy system] was to block X-rated materials. You can see the first pages [of sexually explicit sites], but not whatever is after that.

The official added that although Etisalat blocks attempts to access proscribed material, authorities do not track individual users' online activities. However, such monitoring, if it ever were to be conducted, would be facilitated by the fact that all dial-in users are channeled through a proxy server operated by a public utility.

The same official acknowledged that the proxy filtering system was not foolproof. "You can get to porno," he said, "because you can always just dial a foreign server. We try our best to limit x-rated material, but you can never really build a wall." Other officials interviewed by Human Rights Watch concurred and added that the proxy server prevents access only for users with dial-up service. Users who connect via a dedicated line—found primarily in workplaces—access the Internet directly, bypassing the censorship imposed by the proxy server.

An official at Etisalat, who also asked not to be named, told Human Rights Watch in a June 18, 1998 telephone interview that the proxy system is maintained in collaboration with a U.S. firm that is contracted to maintain and update the filtering software that is run by the proxy server. The Etisalat staff reviews web sites, sometimes responding to complaints or tips from users, and informs the U.S. company of material they wish to block. The official refused to disclose the name of the U.S. company, or provide the criteria used to determine which sites are blocked. Etisalat provides the U.S. company with "broad guidelines," he explained, for rooting out objectionable sites. Denying that this included political or cultural sites, he said the "guidelines we've passed along are fairly basic." They focus on the "sexually explicit."

An information systems manager who worked for Etisalat when the proxy server system was being developed in the mid-1990s told Human Rights Watch in a June 9, 1998 telephone interview that the system was set up in response to concerns that "there was a great deal of misuse [of the Internet] among teenagers." To complement the filtering done by the U.S. company, Etisalat "got a program running with parents, or with whomever finds [an objectionable] site, so that the person will inform Etisalat and then Etisalat restricts it. There's a committee of technical people at Etisalat who look at the site, and verify it has nude pictures, and then they stop it."

While all of the Emirati officials we interviewed insisted that the proxy server exists only to block pornography, Human Rights Watch identified at least one blocked site that is cultural and political in nature. It is the site of the Gay and

Lesbian Arabic Society (<www.glas.org>). When asked about the site, the Information and Culture Ministry official quoted above acknowledged that it was blocked, explaining, "We got complaints about it."

GLAS describes itself in its web site as:

> a networking organization for Gay and Lesbians of Arab descent or those living in Arab countries. We aim to promote positive images of Gays and Lesbians in Arab communities worldwide. We also provide a support network for our members while fighting for our human rights wherever they are oppressed. We are part of the global Gay and Lesbian movement seeking an end to injustice and discrimination based on sexual orientation.

The GLAS web site hosts a chat-line, and reports and editorializes on such topics as AIDS, asylum cases involving gays and transsexuals, civil marriages in Lebanon, and the imprisonment of political dissidents in the region. In May of 1998, GLAS proclaimed on its web site:

> We are also keeping track of flagrant human rights violations in Gulf countries and particularly in the U.A.E. where recent deportation of HIV patients has made headlines....Such activities need to be denounced at every occasion. The U.A.E. puts a lot of effort at presenting itself as a major business center in the area. The message should be sent that human rights violations will not be ignored and that we will make sure their image continues to be tarnished and their violations denounced.

Human Rights Watch is unaware of web sites belonging to governments or political movements that are blocked in the U.A.E. However, the blocking of the GLAS site indicates that Internet censorship in the U.A.E. exceeds the proclaimed goal of restricting pornography.

The U.A.E. government did not reply in writing to the list of questions submitted by Human Rights Watch to all governments of the region. It did however invite Human Rights Watch to the U.A.E. Embassy in Washington to discuss Internet issues. In addition, officials in the Ministry of Information and Culture and another at Etisalat proved willing to answer some questions during telephone interviews with Human Rights Watch; they are cited above.

At the embassy meeting, held on July 10, 1998, political counselor Abdullah al-Saleh and legal advisor Mohamed Mattar explained that Internet users enjoyed considerable freedom in the U.A.E., and pointed to constitutional guarantees of free expression and of privacy. Article 30 of the U.A.E. Constitution states, "Freedom of opinion and expressing it verbally, in writing or by other means of expression shall be guaranteed within the limits of law." Article 31 states, "Freedom of communication by post, telegraph or other means of communication and the secrecy thereof shall be guaranteed in accordance with the law." Mattar suggested that the references in these articles to "other means" presumably extended to the Internet. Similarly, the 1991 law on telecommunications, which affirms the application of criminal law statutes (such as with respect to fraud) to the realm of telecommunications, would apply to conduct on the Internet. He stated that the U.A.E. had no Internet-specific legislation.

Al-Saleh added that the U.A.E.'s only intervention with regard to Internet use concerns the blocking of web sites. He said the state does not interfere with or conduct surveillance of e-mail. There have been no arrests, he said, of persons for any kind of "misuse" of the Internet. Human Rights Watch has received no information that contradicts his assertions. However, Maj. Gen. Dhahi Khalfan Tamim, the Chief of Police of Dubai, one of the seven constituent emirates of the U.A.E., publicly advocated police oversight of the Internet. In 1996, for example, h was quoted in the press as saying that the Ministry of Information and the police, rather than Etisalat, should be responsible for licensing Internet use. "In all cases, the information should be filtered, scanned and then made available to users," the *Gulf News* quoted him as saying.[135] Asked for comment on Tamim's proposal to give the police and information ministry oversight of the Internet, the Information and Culture Ministry official quoted above wrote to Human Rights Watch on June 16, 1998 that this had never been implemented and merely represented "his [the police chief's] point of view."

The same official also stated that all web sites must be registered with the Ministry of Information. "But this is just a formality; we've never denied any request, and don't think we ever will. We do not monitor the material. It's just to make sure it's a real company," to prevent commercial fraud and copyright infringements.

---

[135] "Dubai: Emirates Telecoms Group, Police in Internet Row," Reuters, June 18, 1996.

APPENDIX A
Table showing Internet use in the Middle East

The following table and accompanying text is reprinted from the web site of Nua, Ltd. (<www.nua.ie/surveys/how_many_online>), an information technology company that publishes numerous surveys of Internet use.

How Many Online?

The art of estimating how many are online throughout the world is an inexact one at best. Surveys abound, using all sorts of measurement parameters. However, from observing many of the published surveys over the last two years, here is an 'educated guess' as to how many are online worldwide as of May 1999. And the number is 165 million.

World Total 165 million
  Africa: 1.14 million
  Asia/Pacific: 26.97 million
  Europe: 40.09 million
  Middle East: 0.88 million
  Canada & USA: 90.63 million
  South America: 5.29 million

A note on survey methodology

- 'How Many Online' figures represent both adults and children who have accessed the Internet at least once during the 3 months prior to being surveyed.
- An Internet User represents a person with access to the Internet and is not specific to Internet Account holders. When the figure for Internet Account holders is the only information available, this figure is multiplied by a factor of 3 to give the number of Internet users.
- The figure for 'Asia/Pacific' includes Australia and New Zealand.
- When more than one survey is available on a country's demographics, Nua will take the mean of the two surveys or, in the case where Nua feels one study may be more comprehensive/reliable than the other, Nua will quote this figure over the other.

71

Middle East: How Many Online?

COUNTRY	DATE	NUMBER	% TOT POP.	SOURCE
U.A.E.	January 1998	88,552	2.99	DIT Group
U.A.E.	July 1997	45,150	1.47	DIT Group
Bahrain & Saudi Arabia	January 1998	46,538	0.23	DIT Group
Bahrain & Saudi Arabia	July 1997	38,480	0.19	DIT Group
Israel	January 1999	600,000	10.8	IDC Research
Israel	May 1998	300,000	5.5	Internet Israel
Jordan	January 1998	20,213	0.50	DIT Group
Jordan	July 1997	11,840	0.28	DIT Group
Kuwait	January 1998	42,350	2.15	DIT Group
Kuwait	July 1997	29,600	1.51	DIT Group
Lebanon	January 1998	43,828	1.14	DIT Group
Lebanon	July 1997	35,520	0.95	DIT Group
Oman	January 1998	20,888	0.95	DIT Group
Oman	July 1997	11,425	0.52	DIT Group
Qatar	January 1998	17,295	3.10	DIT Group
Qatar	July 1997	8,265	1.51	DIT Group
Yemen	December 1997	2426	-	DIT Group

APPENDIX B: Uniform letter requesting information on Internet policies, sent by Human Rights Watch in May 1999 to governments of the region

HUMAN RIGHTS WATCH
1522 K Street, NW #910
Washington, DC 20005
Telephone: (202) 371-6592
Facsimile: (202)371-0124
E-mail: goldstr@hrw.org
Website: http://www.hrw.org

MIDDLE EAST AND NORTH AFRICA DIVISION
Hanny Megally
Executive Director
Eric Goldstein
Research Director
Virginia N. Sherry
Associate Director
Joe Stork
Advocacy Director
Clarisa Bencomo
Elahé Sharifpour-Hicks
Nejla Sammakia
Research Associates
Georgina Copty
Awali Samara
Associates
ADVISORY COMMITTEE
Gary G. Sick
Chair
Lisa Anderson
Bruce Rabb
Vice Chairs
Khaled Abou El-Fadl
Shaul Bakhash
M. Cherif Bassiouni
Martin Blumenthal
Paul Chevigny
Helena Cobban
Edith Everett
Mansour Farhang
Christopher E. George
Rita E. Hauser
Ulrich Haynes
Rev. J. Bryan Hehir
Edy Kaufman
Marina Pinto Kaufman
Samir Khalaf
Judith Kipper
Ann M. Lesch
Stephen P. Marks
Rolando Matalon
Philip Mattar
Jean-Francois Seznec
Charles Shamas
David K. Shipler
Sanford Solender
Mary Ann Stein
Shibley Telhami
Andrew Whitley
Napoleon B. Williams, Jr.
James J. Zogby
HUMAN RIGHTS WATCH
Kenneth Roth
Executive Director
Michele Alexander
Development Director
Carroll Bogert
Communications Director
Reed Brody
Advocacy Director, NY
Cynthia Brown
Program Director
Barbara Guglielmo
*Finance & Administration
Director*
Susan Osnos
Associate Director
Wilder Tayler
General Counsel
Lotte Leicht
Brussels Office Director
Joanna Weschler
*United Nations
Representative*
Jonathan Fanton, *Chair*

May 19, 1998

H.E. Ambassador Ahmed Maher El Sayed
Embassy of the Arab Republic of Egypt
3521 International Court, NW
Washington, D.C. 20008

Dear Ambassador El Sayed:

Human Rights Watch is preparing a report on the spread of the Internet in the countries of the Middle East and North Africa. As an independent, nonpartisan human rights organization, we shall apply internationally recognized principles of freedom of expression to the subject, looking specifically at the freedom that people enjoy in each country to impart and receive information electronically.

To ensure that the report we publish accurately reflects official perspectives, we are sending this open letter to all of the embassies in the U.S. representing Middle Eastern and North African countries.

We would be grateful to receive from you answers to the following questions relating to the Internet in Egypt. All information received by June 15 will be reflected in the report, which Human Rights Watch expects to publish this summer. Please do not hesitate to contact me if you have any questions.

[1] LAWS. Are there laws or regulations that govern speech content online (e.g., electronic mail, newsgroups, chat forums, online discussions, websites, and other forums on the Internet)? If so, can you provide us with a copy of that legislation, or indicate where the text[s] may be found? Is online speech subject to the press code or information code in effect in Egypt?

[2] ACCESS. Are individuals, organizations, and corporations permitted to establish accounts with Internet Service Providers (ISPs), so that they can obtain access to the Internet through a domestic telephone call?

[3] REGISTRATION WITH GOVERNMENT. What information, if any, are individuals or organizations or corporations required to furnish to government agencies before (a) obtaining Internet access? (b) posting a website?

[4] GOVERNMENT APPROVAL. Is any sort of approval from a government agency required before an individual, organization, or corporation may (a) have Internet access? (b) post a website?

[5] CONFIDENTIALITY. Are ISPs required to provide to the authorities information about their subscribers or users, or about the content of their Internet activities? If so, what type of information, and under what conditions are they required to turn over such information?

[6] ENCRYPTION. Is there legislation regulating the use of encryption in electronic communication?

[7] CONTENT REGULATIONS. Do authorities mandate, or require ISPs to mandate, regulations on speech content or information that is sent or received by Internet users? If so, please describe those regulations and the penalties for violating them.

[8] "BLOCKING" AND CENSORSHIP. Do authorities block or censor the content of any websites or of electronic communications via newsgroups, e-mail or other Internet forums?

If so, what are the criteria used to determine material that is blocked or censored, and by what methods (e.g., proxy servers, fire walls, filtering software, buffers) is it achieved?

[9] LIABILITY. Are there laws that hold an ISP (or data carriers) responsible for the content of e-mail messages, websites, or newsgroup postings that are transmitted by others (content providers) via that ISP?

[10] "CYBER-CAFES" AND LIBRARIES. Are there regulations governing the operation of locations (such as cyber-cafés and libraries) where members of the public can have access to the Internet?

Are those responsible for such facilities required to furnish any government agency with information about the users and use of their facilities?

Are they considered legally responsible for material that is sent from, or received at, their premises?

[11] INEXPENSIVE ACCESS. Does your government have any programs in place to help make Internet access easy and affordable to the general public?

Please feel free to add or send any additional information about the Internet that is pertinent. Once again, please contact me if you have questions, or desire further information, about this project or about any aspect of Human Rights Watch. I would be happy to send you our 1996 report on the Internet, as well as any of our publications concerning the Middle East and North Africa.

Thank you for your cooperation.

Sincerely yours,

Eric Goldstein
Research Director
Middle East and North Africa Division
Human Rights Watch

APPENDIX C: Replies to Human Rights Watch letter received from officials of Iraq, Jordan, Kuwait, Qatar, Tunisia and Yemen

Permanent Mission Of Iraq

To The United Nations

14 East, 79th Street
New York, N.Y. 10021
Tel : (212) 737-4433
Fax : (212) 772-1794

مَثِيلةجمهوريّةِالعِراقِالدائمة
لدَى الأُمم المُتحِدة
نــيـويورك

هاتف : (٢١٢)٧٣٧-٤٤٣٣
فاكس : (٢١٢)٧٧٢-١٧٩٤

June 1, 1998

Mr. Eric Goldstein
Human Rights Watch

Dear Mr. Goldstein,

Thank you for your letter of May 21, 1998 in which you are seeking information about the freedom of expression and the Internet in Iraq. I am afraid to say that your understanding that Iraq has no connection to the Internet was correct. This was due to the vast damage effected the infrastructure in Iraq, particularly the communications network during the military aggression on Iraq in 1991, as well as the serious impacts of the on going comprehensive blockade which has been imposed on Iraq since 1990. Moreover, Iraq is prohibited from having the requirements for spare parts to this sector within the framework of the Memorandum of Understanding.

As regards to the comments of Iraq on the Internet as it relates to the right of persons to receive and disseminate information. We understand that this right is a part of freedom of opinion, which is guaranteed by the Iraqi Constitution. Article 26 stipulates that: The Constitution guarantees freedom of opinion, publication and assembly and also freedom to hold demonstrations and to establish political parties, trade unions and associations in conformity with the aims of the Constitution and within the limits of the Law. The state shall endeavor to provide the facilities needed for the exercise of this freedom.

Sincerely Yours,

Nizar Hamdoon
Ambassador
Permanent Representative

EMBASSY OF THE HASHEMITE KINGDOM OF JORDAN
WASHINGTON, D.C.

May 21, 1998

Mr. Eric Goldstein
Research Director
Middle East and North Africa Division
Human Rights Watch
1522 K St. NW
Washington, D.C. 20005

Dear Mr Goldstein,

Thank you for you letter of May 19, 1998. I hope the following answers your questions on the Internet and its use in Jordan. I have tried to respond directly to each of the questions posed in your correspondence.

1. Laws: There are no laws that govern speech content online in Jordan

2. Access: All individuals, organizations and corporations are permitted to establish accounts with ISP's, obtaining access through a domestic telephone call. Presently, there are eight licenses awarded, and three private-sector companies providing access to the internet in Jordan.

3. Registration with government: No information is required to be furnished to the government before obtaining internet access or posting a website.

4. Government Approval: No government approval from a government agency is required for internet access or posting a website.

5. Confidentiality. No information is required by the government from ISPs relating to the content of their internet activities.

6. Encryption: There is no legislation regulating the use of encryption in electronic communication.

7. Content Regulation: There are no content regulations by the government.

EMBASSY OF THE HASHEMITE KINGDOM OF JORDAN
WASHINGTON, D.C.

8. Blocking and censorship: There is no blocking or censoring by the government of the content of any websites or of electronic communications via newsgroups, e-mail or other Internet forums.

9. Liability: There are no laws that hold ISP's responsible for the content of e-mail messages, websites, or newsgroup postings that are transmitted by others.

10. Cyber-cafes and libraries: There are cyber-cafes in Jordan. There are no special laws relating to their operation other than the standard licensees they have to obtain as any other business.

11. Inexpensive Access: His Majesty has recently announced a program to provide free internet services to all public schools. Internet access rates are determined by the market. All internet providers in Jordan with the exception of one are private-sector companies.

　　　　I hope the above answers your questions. Please feel free to contact me for any additional information you might require.

Sincerely,

Marwan Muasher
Ambassador

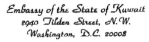

Embassy of the State of Kuwait
2940 Tilden Street, N.W.
Washington, D.C. 20008

سَفـــارة دَولَةِ الكُوَيْت
واشـــنطن

12th August 1998

Mr. Eric Goldstein
Research Director
Middle East and North Africa Division
Human Rights Watch

Dear Mr. Goldstein,

I hope your research and final report on *"The Spread of the Internet in the Countries of the Middle East and Africa"* is moving along smoothly.

In regards to your letter, dated May 19th 1998, inquiring about Internet access in Kuwait, I have the following to report:

LAWS - There are no laws or regulations in Kuwait that govern free speech online at this moment. The Printing and Publications Law of the Ministry of Information, therefore, does not apply to the Internet. Nevertheless, further studies might be conducted to have this law include the Internet, depending on new developments in the international arena.

Again, I wish you the best on your report. If you have any further inquiries on this matter, please do not hesitate to contact me.

Sincerely,

Amer Ali Al-Mutairi
Diplomatic Attache

EMBASSY OF THE
STATE OF QATAR
Washington D.C.

سفارة دولة قطر

واشنطن دي.سي.

Ref: 173/9/98
Date: September 22,1998

Mr. Eric Goldstein
Research Director
Middle East and North Africa Division
Human Rights Watch

In response to your letter of May 19th 1998, please find enclosed copies of
the Rules and Regulations that govern the internet services in the State of
Qatar.

We appreciate your interest in our country.

Best Regards

Sincerely,

Saad Mohamed Al-Kobaisi
Ambassador

(كيوتل) المؤسسة العامة القطرية للاتصالات السلكية واللاسلكية
Qatar Public Telecommunications Corporation (Q.TEL)

TERMS & CONDITIONS

1 ▬ Definitions
1.1 *Internet Qatar*: The Internet Service provided solely by Qatar Public Telecommunications Corporation (Q-Tel). It will here-after be called the "service".
1.2 *The customer*: Any Individual, Company, Corporation or any other entity subscribing to the service.
1.3 *Contract* : Internet Qatar Application form signed by the customer.

2 ▬ Access and Services:
2.1 *Dial-Up Access*: A user name and a password will be assigned to the customer, who shall use his own means (e.g. comput-er telephone service and modem) to connect to the service.
2.2 *Dedicated Access*: A local leased line will be installed for the customer, who shall use his own router and other equipment to establish physical connection to access the service.
2.3 *Optional Web service*: A disk space on Q-Tel's servers will be allocated to the customer for publishing information through web pages.

3 ▬ Use:
3.1 The customer shall, at all times, protect the secrecy of the password assigned to him. The customer shall be fully re-sponsible and shall be also charged, for losses, damages arising from any use of this user name and password. The cus-tomer shall change his password from time to time to guarantee security.
3.2 The customer shall not use the service to:
3.2.1 Infringe any copyright or intellectual property rights to any information or resources.
3.2.2 Without lawful excuse, send messages which cause or may cause any threat, harassment, annoyance, inconvenience or needless anxiety to any person.
3.2.3 Attempt or gain access to any computer system or to any private information or resources without the written approval of t owners of the right of such system, information or resources.
3.2.4 To commit any criminal or illegal act or to achieve any unlawful purpose, including but not limited to, gambling or obscenity or to carry out any activity which is contrary to public order.
3.2.5 Provide public information services without obtaining formal approval from the relevant government authorities within the State of Qatar.
3.3 The customer shall:
3.3.1 Be responsible for the data transmitted, stored or retrieved through the service.
3.3.2 Be responsible for managing the space allocated to him.
3.3.3 Pay Q-Tel the monthly services charges on timely basis.
3.4 The customer shall not be entitled to trade on connectivity, resell, hire, transfer, assign or otherwise dispose of the service without the prior written approval of Q-Tel.

4 ▬ Any breach or violation of any of these conditions and any misuse of the service shall be at the sole risk and cost of the cus-tomer. The customer shall indemnify and hold harmless Q-Tel against any liability that it may suffer as a result of any such breach.

5 ▬ Q-Tel shall not guarantee any specific response time for any method of access to the service.

6 ▬ The charges for the service shall be based on tariff published by Q-Tel and any amendments thereto as maybe introduced by Q-Tel from time to time.

7 ▬ Q-Tel shall have the right to obtain a deposit from the customer and the customer shall be bound to refurbish such deposit up to the limit determined by Q-Tel whenever the amount of the deposit becomes less than the prescribed limit.

8 ▬ Software
8.1 The customer may use the software supplied by Q-Tel in addition to other software not owned or supplied by Q-Tel. The use of such additional software shall be subject to the terms and conditions herein stated shall be at the sole risk and re-sponsibility of the customer.
8.2 Q-Tel makes no warranty and shall not be responsible or liable to the customer for any losses or damages whosoever aris-ing out of the use of software provided to the customer. The customer or any third party shall have no right or claim against Q-Tel for any defects in the software. In no event will Q-Tel be liable to the customer for any damages whatsoever, including any loss of profits, loss of savings, or other incidental or consequential damages arising out of the customer's use or inability to use the software even if Q-Tel or any of its authorized representative has been advised of the possibility of any defects in the software.
8.3 The customer shall satisfy himself as to the suitability of the software for his needs. The customer shall also be responsible for ensuring the compatibility of the software with his equipment.
8.4 In the event that changes are introduced to Q-Tel's Network, Q-Tel shall not be responsible to ensure that the software will continue to be compatible with Q-Tel's Network and the customer shall have no claim whatsoever against Q-Tel for any losses or damage of any kind whosoever which he may suffer as a result of such changes.
8.5 The customer shall strictly comply, and shall ensure compliance by his servants and agents, with all instructions or notices in whatever form and through whatever means given by Q-Tel from time to time regarding the use of the software.

9 ▬ Termination:
9.1 Q-Tel may suspend or terminate the service for non-payment or delay in payment by the customer of any amounts due to Q-Tel. Non-receipt of bills will not be considered an acceptable reason to delay the payment of these dues.
9.2 Q-Tel may suspend or terminate Internet Qatar service if charges for other services provided by Q-Tel to the same customer become overdue; and may suspend or terminate other services provided by Q-Tel to the same customer if charges for Inter-net Qatar services become overdue.
9.3 Q-Tel may suspend or terminate the service if the customer breaches or violates any of the conditions stated in condition 3 or any other condition herein stated and may suspend or terminate the service for any other reasons it sees fit.

10 ▬ Q-Tel may, at any time, introduce any amendments it sees appropriate to these terms and conditions and to any agreement it may conclude with the customer, including the increase of charges. The customer may not object to such amendments and shall be bound thereby on the advent of the effective date specified by Q-Tel.

11 ▬ In cases not provided for by these terms and conditions, the general terms and conditions for Telecommunication services shall apply.

EMBASSY OF THE
STATE OF QATAR
Washington D.C.

سفارة دولة قطر
واشنطن دي.سي.

Mr. Eric Goldstein   Ref.: 203/98
Human Rights Watch
1522 K. Street N.W.
Washington, DC 20005

Dear Mr. Goldstein,

Reference to your letter dated October 16, 1998 concerning the rules and regulations governing Internet Services in the State of Qatar. Please find attached an unofficial translation for Articles 3.2.4 and 3.2.5 .

Embassy of the State of Qatar
Washington, DC
November 25, 1998

UNOFFICIAL TRANSLATION

(a) "All Internet users should comply with the rules of public order. This compliance is a public commitment and should be duly respected by all people living in the State of Qatar in accordance with Article (15) of the amended provisional Regulatory Act. There is no concise definite context of the phrase "public order" but it refers in general to the necessity of commitment to the State's public policies and to the community's traditions and values."

(b) "All services provided by Qatar Public Telecommunications Corporation (Q.Tel.) such as telephone services. The internet system avails the possibility of telephone communications and Q.Tel. is keen that such communications should not be commercially misused by subscribers. To this effect, it has been ruled that such "public service" as the internet telephone communications shall not be provided without the approval of the relevant government authority- Q.Tel. This is considered as a normal procedure to protect the public services of Q.Tel."

EMBASSY OF TUNISIA
1515 MASSACHUSETTS AVENUE, N. W.
WASHINGTON, D. C. 20005

June 12, 1998

Mr. Eric Goldstein
Research Director
Middle East and North Africa Division
Human Rights Watch
1522 K Street, NW
Washington, DC 20005

Dear Mr. Goldstein: Eric

Further to your letter of May 1998 regarding the Internet in Tunisia, I am pleased to enclose, herewith, a document containing answers to your questions.

This document is presently available only in French. However if it is necessary to have it in English, we will be glad to translate it.

I look forward to hearing from you in the near future.

Best Regards,

Nejmeddine Lakhal
First Secretary

1 - LOIS

QUESTION

Y a-t-il des lois ou des règlements qui régissent le contenu de l'expression en ligne (par exemple, courrier électronique, newsgroups, forum de discussion, discussions en ligne), si oui, pouvez-vous nous en fournir une copie ou nous indiquer où ces textes peuvent être trouvés ?

L'expression en ligne est-elle soumise au code de la presse ou au code de l'information en vigueur en Tunisie ?

REPONSE

Pour promouvoir les services à valeur ajoutée des télécommunications, et en particulier les services de type Internet, et dans l'optique de préparer la Tunisie à l'ère de la société de l'information, un cadre global a été mis en place couvrant les aspects liés à l'infrastructure des télécommunications, aux fournisseurs de services Internet, à la politique tarifaire et au domaine réglementaire.

Le cadre réglementaire est constitué par le décret n°97-501 en date du 14 Mars 1997 relatif aux services à valeur ajoutée des télécommunications (Journal Officiel de la République Tunisienne n°24, de 1997), incluant les services Internet ainsi que les arrêtés relatifs à la tarification et à l'exploitation de ces services (Journal Officiel de la République Tunisienne n°25 de 1997).

Ce cadre réglementaire a pour objectifs de :

- Fournir l'accès aux Services Internet à tous ceux qui le demandent, avec la même qualité et le même prix, à travers tout le pays aussi bien dans les zones urbaines que rurales ;

- Stimuler le secteur privé dans le cadre d'une concurrence loyale pour commercialiser les services d'accès à Internet et développer les capacités d'hébergement des sites web;

- Garantir un niveau de qualité des prestations de services, compatible avec les besoins des utilisateurs à travers des conditions d'exploitation technico-commerciales, mises à la charge des fournisseurs de services Internet ;

- Etablir une politique tarifaire permettant, au large public, d'accéder aux services Internet.

Cette réglementation ne touche pas le contenu de l'expression en ligne à travers : la messagerie électronique, les news groups, les forums de discussion et les discussions en ligne.

Toutefois, le code de la presse et la loi sur la propriété littéraire et artisrique sont applicables aux propriétaires des sites web en Tunisie et aux fournisseurs de services Internet chargés de l'hébergement de ces sites.

2 - ACCES

QUESTION

Est-ce que les individus, les organismes et les sociétés sont autorisés à ouvrir des comptes d'accès avec les fournisseurs de services Internet (ISPs), de sorte qu'ils puissent obtenir l'accès à l'Internet par un appel téléphonique national ?

REPONSE

Oui, à travers le fournisseur de services Internet de leur choix.

3 - DECLARATION AUPRES DU GOUVERNEMENT

QUESTION

Quelle information, si elle existe, les individus, les organismes ou les sociétés doivent fournir aux organismes gouvernementaux avant de (a) obtenir l'accès Internet ? (b) diffuser un site web ?

REPONSE

a - L'accès des individus, des organismes et des sociétés aux services Internet se fait sur simple demande formulée auprès du fournisseur de services Internet de leur choix .
La demande d'accès n'est pas soumise à une déclaration préalable auprès d'un organisme gouvernemental ;

b - La diffusion de sites web ne nécessite pas de déclaration préalable auprès d'un organisme gouvernemental.

4 - APPROBATION DU GOUVERNEMENT

QUESTION

Est-ce que l'approbation d'un organisme gouvernemental est exigée avant qu'un individu,une organisation, ou une société puisse (a) avoir l'accès à Internet ? (b) diffuser un site web ?

REPONSE

> *a - Non*
> *b - Non*

5 - CONFIDENTIALITE

QUESTION

Est-ce que les fournisseurs de services Internet sont tenus de fournir des informations aux autorités au sujet de leurs abonnés ou utilisateurs, ou sur le contenu de leurs activités Internet ? Si oui, quel type d'information, et dans quelles conditions sont-ils tenus de transférer une telle information ?

REPONSE

Pour les besoins de la statistique nationale, seules les informations de base nécessaires en particulier à l'établissement d'annuaires publics des utilisateurs, sont collectées auprès des fournisseurs de services Internet. Toute autre information au sujet des utilisateurs ou de leur activité est obligatoirement gardée confidentielle par les fournisseurs de services Internet.

6 - CRYPTAGE

QUESTION

Y a-t-il une législation régissant l'utilisation du cryptage dans la transmission électronique ?

REPONSE

Oui, le cryptage est régi par l'arrêté du Ministre des Communications en date du 9 Septembre 1997 (Journal Officiel de la République Tunisienne n°76).

7 - REGLEMENTATION SUR LE CONTENU

QUESTION

Les autorités obligent-elles, ou demandent-elles aux fournisseurs de services Internet le respect d'une réglementation sur le contenu de l'information envoyée ou reçue par les utilisateurs d'Internet ? Si oui, prière décrire cette réglementation et les sanctions de sa violation.

REPONSE

Il n'y a d'obligations à respecter que celles qui découlent des textes législatifs en vigueur et en rapport avec la matière considérée (bonnes moeurs, respect de la vie privée, respect des personnes etc. ...)

8 - « BLOCAGE » ET CENSURE

QUESTION

Est ce que les autorités bloquent ou censurent le contenu des sites web ou des communications électroniques établies par l'intermédiaire des newsgroups, de l'E-mail ou d'autres forum sur Internet ?
Si oui, quel est le critère employé pour déterminer la matière à bloquer ou à censurer et quelle est la méthode utilisée à cet effet (par exemple, serveurs proxy, firewalls, logiciels de filtrage, mémoires tampon) ?.

REPONSE

La Tunisie est attachée au principe de la préservation des valeurs morales et la protection de la vie privée des personnes. Les sites Web ou les communications électroniques et alliés sur Internet qui ne tiennent pas compte de ces principes (Pédophilie, pornographie, etc..) sont en infraction avec la législation.
Par ailleurs, la Tunisie suit avec intérêt les débats afférents à cette question, à l'échelle internationale, pour la recherche de solutions appropriées.

9 - RESPONSABILITE

QUESTION

Y a t-il des lois qui tiennent un fournisseur de services Internet (ou transporteur d'information) responsable du contenu des messages E-mail, des sites web, ou des messages newsgroup transmis par d'autres (fournisseurs de contenu) via cet ISP ?

REPONSE

Non, toutefois les ISP sont responsables uniquement du contenu des sites web qu'ils hébergent.

10 - CYBER-CAFES BIBLIOTHEQUES

QUESTION

Y a-t-il des règlements régissant la mise en place d'emplacements (tels que le cyber-cafés et les bibliothèques) ‹ le public peut avoir accès à l'Internet ?
Est-ce que ceux-ci sont tenus de fournir à un organisme ou à une agence gouvernementale des informations sur les utilisateurs et l'utilisation de leurs équipements ?
Sont-ils considérés légalement responsables de la matière informationnelle envoyée ou reçue sur leurs lieux ?

REPONSE

Plutôt que de Cyber-Cafés, il est préférable de parler de Cyber- espace; autrement dit d'un espace permettant au public d'accéder à Internet.

La Tunisie a une politique claire et ambitieuse en matière de connexion du plus grand nombre de ses citoyens à l'Internet. C'est ainsi , qu'outre la facilité et la rapidité d'accès offerte à l'échelle individuelle, un ambitieux programme est en cours de réalisation. Il vise la connexion du réseau Internet de toutes les institutions universitaires et de recherche scientifique, la connexion des lycées et collèges devant suivre par étapes, d'ici la fin du plan actuel (l'an 2001) avec la perspective de relier les écoles primaires à ce réseau dans l'étape suivante.

Parallèlement, des Clubs Informatiques avec connexion progressive au réseau d'Internet sont en cours d'installation à travers toutes les régions du pays. Certains sont l'oeuvre d'associations culturelles et éducatives. De même, il a été décidé de connecter l'ensemble des bibliothèques publiques. Si bien que des Cyber espaces existent et seront progressivement généralisés à l'ensemble du territoire national. C'est l'approche qui a été retenue.

11 - ACCES PEU COUTEUX

QUESTION

Votre gouvernement a-t-il des programmes en place aidant à rendre l'accès Internet facile et accessible au grand public ?

REPONSE

Dans le but de rendre l'accès aux services Internet facile et à la portée du grand public en Tunisie, plusieurs décisions gouvernementales ont été prises ces dernières années pour la mise en oeuvre d'actions concourant à la satisfaction de cet objectif.

Premièrement, concernant l'infrastructure du réseau Internet, la bande passante entre la Tunisie et le réseau mondial de l'Internet est passée à 5 Mbit/s et atteindra à la fin de cette année 8 Mbit/s. Il est important d'indiquer que la bande passante était de 512 Kbit/s, il y a seulement une année.

Par ailleurs, l'épine dorsale nationale de l'Internet (Back-bone) exploitant des liaisons en fibres optiques à hauts débits, est actuellement en cours de mise en place pour couvrir l'ensemble des régions de la Tunisie et écouler un trafic issu de besoins en pleine croissance.

Deuxièmement, plusieurs fournisseurs de services Internet ont été chargés de commercialiser les services d'accès à Internet et de couvrir les besoins des utilisateurs potentiels, les institutions gouvernementales, les institutions d'enseignement et d'éducation, les établissements de recherche, les entreprises économiques ainsi que les particuliers.

Il est demandé à ces fournisseurs de contribuer au processus de développement de l'Internet en Tunisie et sa vulgarisation auprès du grand public.

Troisièmement, son Excellence le Président de la République Tunisienne Zine El Abidine BEN ALI a instruit le gouvernement de mener une étude prospective sur "l'école de demain" à la lumière de l'évolution mondiale vers la société de l'information, et d'engager un programme de généralisation de l'introduction de technologie de l'information et en particulier d'Internet dans toutes les universités, les centres de recherches, les lycées secondaires durant le 9ème Plan 1997-2001 et les écoles primaires ultérieurement et par étapes.

Quatrièmement, les tarifs de connexion à Internet ont fait l'objet de multiples réductions, dans le but de rendre la connexion Internet plus abordable au grand public. Actuellement, le tarif mensuel d'une connexion Internet est de l'ordre de 30 dinars (25$ US dollars) avec un accès illimité, comparé aux 125 DT (115$ US dollars) l'année dernière.

D'autre part, le tarif de communication téléphonique, pour l'accès aux services Internet, a été considérablement réduit pour atteindre 30 millimes/minute pendant la journée et 20 millimes/minute la nuit. Ces tarifs étaient jusqu'au 30 Avril 1998, de 70 millimes/minute pendant la journée et 40 millimes/minute la nuit.

Cinquièmement, il y a lieu de signaler que l'importation en Tunisie d'équipements micro-informatiques par les entreprises ou les particuliers bénéficie d'avantages fiscaux particuliers à même de favoriser la généralisation de l'utilisation informatique à l'échelle du pays.

EMBASSY OF
THE REPUBLIC OF YEMEN
SUITE 705
2600 VIRGINIA AVENUE, N.W.
WASHINGTON, D.C. 20037
TEL:(202) 965-4760
FAX:(202) 337-2017

سفارة الجمهورية اليمنية
بواشنطن

May 26, 1998

Eric Goldstein
Research Director
Middle East and North Africa Division
Human Rights Watch
1522 K Street, NW# 910
Washington, D.C. 20005.

Dear Sir,

It is my honor to acknowledge the receipt of your letter of May 19, 1998 addressed to H.E.
Ambassador Abdulwahab A. Al-Hajjri who is currently in Yemen. However, due to the technical and
legislative nature of your question, I would like to encourage you to contact the Internet Service
provider in Yemen on the following electronic address: "www.y.net.ye."
Moreover, you will find enclosed a list of some existing Yemeni web sites .

I take this opportunity to thank you again for your interest in Yemen and I am looking forward to
receive a copy of your report on the rights for Internet access in the Middle East and North African
countries.

With my best greeting,

Sincerely yours,
Ahmed Ali Atef
Counselor
Political & Information
Affairs.

Mr Eric Goldstein
Research Director ME and NA Division
Human Rights Watch
1522 K St. NW
Washington DC 20005
USA

Fax: + 1 202 371 0124

8th August 1998

Dear Mr Goldstein,

Your letter of 18th May 1998 to Ambassador Al Hajjri, and the subsequent correspondence with our Deputy General Manager, Mr Ali Basahi, has been passed to me for attention.

As perhaps you may be aware, Teleyemen is the international telecommunications provider for the Republic of Yemen, and within this framework we are also the Internet Service Provider; the service which we offer is branded as "y.net". The questions which you ask will therefore be answered by us. As we are ultimately a public company, our answers have no "official" standing, as we are representing only ourselves.

1. **LAWS.** There are no specific laws which govern materials sent or received on line via the internet. On line materials are not subject to press or information codes.
2. **ACCESS.** The Yemen internet service is a freely available public service. The only constraint which is placed on the establishment of an account with Teleyemen, as the ISP, is that the customer must prove creditworthiness. This is purely an internal financial measure and is not used to classify or restrict access for any other reason. We do not make any distinction between personal, organisational, or corporate customers. All internet access to the "y.net" node is currently by domestic telephone call.
3. **REGISTRATION WITH GOVERNMENT.** No information is required to be submitted to any Governmental, or quasi-Governmental, agency regarding any usage of the internet, either before or after the fact.

4. **GOVERNMENT APPROVAL.** No Governmental approval of any sort is required before any individual, organisation, or corporation, may have Internet access or post a web site.
5. **CONFIDENTIALITY.** No information of any sort is provided by Teleyemen to anyone concerning the subscribers to "y.net", or their activities on the internet, or the content of those activities.
6. **ENCRYPTION.** There is no specific legislation concerning the use of encryption on the internet.
7. **CONTENT REGULATION.** There are no specific regulations regarding the content of information sent or received by internet users.
8. **BLOCKING AND CENSORSHIP.** There is a general requirement on Teleyemen as ISP to limit access to information which is considered to be undesirable in terms of causing offence against social, religious, or cultural standards. We implement this general requirement by the use of the standard "SURFWATCH" system, operated in conjunction with a proxy server. Should we be requested to bar access to a specific site by a competent authority, we would do this, but this is not common practice.
9. **LIABILITY.** There are no specific laws which create a liability on the ISP in respect of the content of transmissions. The standard agreement under which "y.net" service is provided to the customer places the responsibility for observing any legal requirements on the customer.
10. **CYBER CAFES AND LIBRARIES.** There are no specific regulations governing the operation of public-access internet locations. From the ISP viewpoint, there is no difference between a public-access user and any other user.
11. **INEXPENSIVE ACCESS.** There are no programmes to subsidise internet access.

I hope that the above information answers your questions. If there is anything further you need, please let me know. My contact details are as follows:
Office phone: +967 1 271435   Office fax: +967 1 271436   email: cleather@y.net.ye

With kind regards,

Christopher D Leather
Divisional Manager
Commercial, Operations & Marketing

SOCIAL SCIENCE LIBRARY

Manor Road Building
Manor Road
Oxford OX1 3UQ
Tel: (2)71093 (enquiries and renewals)
http://www.ssl.ox.ac.uk

This is a NORMAL LOAN item.

We will email you a reminder before this item is due.

Please see http://www.ssl.ox.ac.uk/lending.html
for details on:

- loan policies; these are also displayed on the notice boards and in our library guide.

- how to check when your books are due back.

- how to renew your books, including information on the maximum number of renewals. Items may be renewed if not reserved by another reader. Items must be renewed before the library closes on the due date.

- level of fines; fines are charged on overdue books.

Please note that this item may be recalled during Term.

305335257X